30 LIFE PRINCIPLES

STUDY GUIDE

A Guide for Growing in Knowledge
and Understanding of God

DR. CHARLES F. STANLEY

Harper*Christian*
Resources

30 Life Principles Study Guide, Revised and Updated
© 2008, 2022 by Dr. Charles F. Stanley

Requests for information should be addressed to:
HarperChristian Resources, 3900 Sparks Dr. SE, Grand Rapids, Michigan 49546

ISBN 978-0-310-14526-4 (softcover)
ISBN 978-0-310-14527-1 (ebook)

HarperChristian Resources titles may be purchased in bulk for church, business, fundraising, or ministry use. For information, please e-mail ResourceSpecialist@ChurchSource.com.

First Printing May 2022 / Printed in the United States of America

CONTENTS

INTRODUCTION

In His Word, God has given you hundreds of life principles to help you become everything that He designed you to be. These are the tenets of faith that have been tried and proven throughout history—truths from the Bible that have never failed and will never disappoint. You can see their impact on the lives of the saints—from Old Testament times to the present day—and God has promised that, if you follow His commands, He will bless your obedience.

During his more than sixty years of ministry, Dr. Charles Stanley has faithfully highlighted the 30 Life Principles that have guided his life and helped him to grow in his knowledge, service, and love of God. Dr. Stanley has taught them so that others can grow into mature followers of the Lord Jesus Christ. Perhaps you've been inspired by these 30 Life Principles and are wondering how you can further make them a part of your life. What does the Bible teach about having a lifetime of spiritual success and avoiding the traps of ineffectiveness and spiritual misery? How do these Life Principles apply to your everyday circumstances and the challenges you face?

This *30 Life Principles Study Guide* has been developed to help you answer these questions and to encourage you in growing in your relationship with Jesus Christ. Of course, these principles were never meant to take the place of God's Word. They are guidelines for discovering the richness of God's truth and knowing God Himself in a deep, intimate relationship. By following these Life Principles, you'll be on the road to the life that He designed for you. And as you submit yourself to Him more fully, God will reveal Himself to you. That's what makes the journey of obedience so exciting.

Of course, it all starts with knowing Jesus Christ as your Lord and Savior. You cannot know God without first knowing the One who reconciles you to Him. Romans 5:10 tells us, "When we were enemies we were reconciled to God through the death of His Son, much more, having been reconciled, we shall be saved by His life." God's Son, Jesus Christ, provides a relationship with Him—and He also provides eternal life if you trust Him. Romans 10:9 promises, "If you confess with your mouth the Lord Jesus and believe in your heart that God has raised Him from the dead, you will be saved."

Would you like to start a personal relationship with God—the One who created you and loves you no matter what? Tell God that you're trusting in Him for salvation. You can tell Him in your own words or use this sample prayer:

Lord Jesus, I know that Your death on the cross was enough to forgive all of my sin and restore my relationship with God. I ask You to forgive my sin and be my Savior. Thank You for providing the way for me to have a growing relationship with my heavenly Father, and thank You for giving me eternal life. I know that You hear my prayers and I praise You for loving me unconditionally and saving me. In Jesus' name, Amen.

If you have just received Christ as your Savior, congratulations! You've just made the very best decision of your life! We would love to know about your decision. Please contact In Touch's Customer Care center at (800) 789-1473, so that we can rejoice with you and send you our *New Believer's Kit* to help you take the next step in your walk with God.

LIFE PRINCIPLE 1

Your Intimacy with God—
His Highest Priority for Your Life—
Determines the Impact of Your Life

*Then God said, "Let Us make man in Our
image, according to Our likeness."*
GENESIS 1:26

Life's Questions

At the beginning of any journey, you must set out in the right direction to reach your destination. This is why this study of Life Principles starts with God's purpose for bringing you into the world. In order to find the life that's worth living, you must understand that you're a special, beloved person and that God has a specific, wonderful plan for you that will give you all the love, fulfillment, significance, and power that you're looking for (see Romans 12:2).

Have you ever wondered what motivated God to design the universe or why He created you? It was *love*—pure and simple. Even before the beginning of the world, God loved you and wanted to have a close, personal relationship with you that would bring great joy, fulfillment, and power to your life (see Ephesians 1:4). Therefore, Life Principle 1 is this: *Your intimacy with God—His highest priority for your life—determines the impact of your life.*

What the Bible Says

1. Read Genesis 1. What did God create before He formed the first man (see verses 1–25)?

2. Why do you think God created all of these things *before* He made people?

3. Why do you think it was important to God to ensure that everything was *good* (see verses 4, 10, 12, 18, 21, 25) before He created mankind (see James 1:17–18)?

The word *good* in the Old Testament also means *well-pleasing, appealing, proper, pleasant to the senses, useful, profitable,* or *a general state of well-being and happiness.* Everything good that comes to you is from God (see James 1:17).

---

4. When God said, "Let Us make man in Our image, according to Our likeness" (Genesis 1:26), what do you think He meant? Why would He want to create someone in His image?

5. What jobs did God give mankind to do (see verses 26–28)? How do our responsibilities relate to the fact that we bear His image?

The word *image* in the Old Testament also means a *likeness, model, semblance,* or *shadow.* This is what you have in common with God and why you can know Him more deeply.

What It Means

Do you wonder what God's will is for your life? He created you in His image for one reason: to have a deep, intimate relationship with you.

God created the world with everything that you would ever need so that you could know and love Him. This means that neither ability, beauty, intelligence, money, nor anything else will ever define your life as successful in God's eyes. It all comes down to how strong your relationship is with Him.

Life Examples

1. Read Genesis 3. What do you think life was like in the Garden of Eden before Adam sinned?

2. Why did Adam disobey God (see verses 5–6)?

When Adam and Eve covered themselves, they did so with fig leaves, which produced sap that would have greatly irritated their skin and made them even more uncomfortable and miserable.

---

3. What was the punishment for Adam's sin (see verses 15–19)? Did their lives become more or less effective after they disobeyed God? Explain.

4. Read John 17:1–5. How would you define eternal life (see verse 3)?

5. Read 1 Corinthians 15:22. How does this verse contrast a life of separation from God with a life of intimacy with God?

Living the Principle

You were created for intimacy with God. The difference your relationship with God makes in your life cannot be overstated. His highest priority for you is to be involved with Him in prayer, the study of His Word, and worship and praise.

Do you want to live a life that is fulfilling and significant? Do you want to make a difference in the world? Then surrender yourself completely to Jesus Christ and ask Him to open your heart to His infinite love and mercy. It's only through your fellowship and communion with God that you can truly affect other people's lives in a way that lasts eternally. Your genuine intimacy with God will become evident in every area of your life, and that will positively affect the influence that you have with every person you encounter.

How will you live out Life Principle 1 this week? Consider some ways that you can pursue a deeper relationship with God. Spend some time with God in prayer, asking Him to draw you into intimate communion with Himself and to transform your life so that you can affect the world for the sake of His kingdom.

Life Lessons to Remember

- God loves you and desires your fellowship and worship (see Deuteronomy 6:5).
- God wants your service for Him to be effective and fruitful (see John 15:5).
- God waits for you to invite Him to bless you (see Revelation 3:20).

LIFE PRINCIPLE 2

Obey God and Leave All the Consequences to Him

"If you will indeed obey My voice and keep My covenant, then you shall be a special treasure to Me above all people."

EXODUS 19:5

Life's Questions

God is the Creator of all that exists. "All things were made through Him, and without Him nothing was made that was made" (John 1:3). As the Creator and Orderer of the universe, He has the power to conform all circumstances to His will. He is also entitled to expect a certain standard of behavior from those who believe in Him.

Of course, such obedience to God can be a challenge, especially when you feel you stand to lose more through your obedience than you might gain. However, when God commands you to obey Him, it's always with your best interests in mind. He knows the outcome of every possible choice you might make and steers you to the path of greatest good.

How do you relate to God, His commands, and the challenges and temptations that confront you each day? When God directs you to do something, how do you respond? Do His commands seem too difficult or costly for you to obey? Are you facing a decision right now that seems overwhelming? Are you torn about whether or not to follow God's instructions? If so, Life Principle 2 should help you: *Obey God and leave all the consequences to Him.*

What the Bible Says

1. Read Exodus 19:1–7. What had happened to the people of Israel in Egypt? (Read Exodus 1 and Psalm 78:43–55 for a summary.)

2. Where were the people of Israel in this passage of Scripture (see verse 2)?

3. Why was it important that the Israelites had seen God's power in action (see verse 4)?

The word *obey* in the Old Testament primarily means *to listen.* It can also mean to *heed, agree, consent, understand,* and *yield to.* To *obey* God means that you listen for His voice and trust what He is telling you. Obeying God is essential to pleasing Him.

4. What was Israel's reward if the people obeyed God (see verses 5–6)?

5. What does it mean to you to be God's "special treasure" (see verse 5)? What especially appeals to you about the promise of His love and acceptance?

What It Means

Before Israel could take over the Promised Land, God had to teach them how to live as His people. His commands were for their benefit and protection so He could establish them in the land and bless them. If they failed to observe God's laws, they would face the terrible consequences of their disobedience (see Deuteronomy 28). The same is true for you. When you disobey God, what you're really saying is you don't have confidence in Him—and you cannot have intimate fellowship with someone you don't trust. But if you're committed to pursuing an intimate relationship with God, trusting and obeying Him in all circumstances, you will know you're receiving His very best—which is far better than you could ever obtain on your own.

Life Examples

1. Read Exodus 3. What was God's command to Moses (see verses 7–10)?

2. What was Moses' initial response to God's command (see verse 11)?

3. What problems and consequences could come about from such a bold move by Moses (see verses 11, 13, 19; see also Exodus 4:1, 10)?

4. Do you think that, humanly speaking, Moses was right to be afraid with all of those obstacles? Why or why not?

5. What was God's specific promise to Moses (see verse 12)? How do you know that God kept His promise?

Horeb and Sinai were two names for the same mountain. Some commentators think that Horeb was the western peak and Sinai was the eastern peak. Others believe one name was for the general mountain range, while the other signified the specific mountain. Either way, we know that God kept His promise.

Living the Principle

The events depicted in Exodus 19 take place on the same mountain where God called Moses to serve Him, which means that God fulfilled His promise to His servant and to Israel. Moses obeyed God despite the consequences that confronted him. As we read in Hebrews 11:27, "By faith he forsook Egypt, not fearing the wrath of the king; for he endured as seeing Him who is invisible." Moses trusted God, and every problem that he faced soon paled in comparison to the mighty love, wisdom, and power of his Commander.

———— ∽ ————

In Exodus 3:14, God said that His name is "I AM WHO I AM." This is also translated as, "I WILL ALWAYS BE WHO I HAVE ALWAYS BEEN," or, "I WILL FOREVER BE WHO I AM NOW." God never changes. As faithful and loving as He was yesterday for Moses, He will also be today, and He will continue to be for all eternity to you (see Hebrews 13:8).

How will you *live out Life Principle 2 this week?* What challenge are you facing today? What is God leading you to do? Your choice in this situation will determine whether you succeed or fail. Therefore, obey God and leave in His hands whatever consequence is causing you to fear. If God makes a promise to you, you can be assured that He will bring it to pass. Spend time in prayer, asking God to draw you into intimate communion with Himself, increase your faith, and transform your life so you can affect the world for the sake of His kingdom.

Life Lessons to Remember

- Trust God with your life and all that concerns you (see Proverbs 3:5–6).
- Wait on the Lord for an answer to your problem or situation (see Psalm 37:9).
- Leave the consequences and outcomes to God (see Exodus 14:13–14).

LIFE PRINCIPLE 3

God's Word Is an Immovable Anchor in Times of Storm

"God is not a man, that He should lie, nor a son of man,
that He should repent. Has He said, and will He not do?
Or has He spoken, and will He not make it good?"
NUMBERS 23:19

Life's Questions

If you've made the decision to seek an intimate relationship with God and obey Him no matter what, you will experience seasons of difficulty and uncertainty. Some challenges you will see coming before they hit. Others will blindside you with the suddenness of a lightning strike. Some challenges that seem manageable at first will prove to be more difficult and serious than you imagined. Others have the potential to turn your life upside down immediately.

Your walk with God is a journey of faith, and there will be situations when your trust in Him will be tested. If you've read the stories of the heroes of the faith in the Bible, you know what a dark night of the soul looks like. Jesus Himself said, "In the world you will have tribulation." But He also added, "Be of good cheer, I have overcome the world" (John 16:33).

What will you cling to when a deluge of trouble rains on your life and everything you know to be true seems to be swept away by intense winds of adversity? What will you hold on to when the waves of doubt threaten to crash down on you? Life Principle 3 holds the answer for you: *God's Word is an immovable anchor in times of storm.*

What the Bible Says

1. Read Numbers 22:1–12. Why were the Moabites afraid of the Israelites (see verses 2–5)?

2. Who was Balaam? What did the Moabites want from him (see verses 6–7)?

The Amorites were a great deal stronger than the Moabites, so when Israel took the Amorite cities so easily (see Numbers 21:21–31), the people of Moab had a good reason to be afraid.

---

3. How did God respond to Balaam (see verse 12)?

4. Read Numbers 22:22–35. When Balaam disobeyed God, how did the Lord get his attention (see verses 28–31)? Why do you think God used such surprising methods?

5. What was the Angel's instruction to Balaam (see verse 35)?

———— ∽◯ ————

Balaam said, "God is not a man, that He should lie, nor a son of man, that He should repent" (Numbers 23:19). When Balaam said that God doesn't *lie,* it means that God will never *fail, deceive,* or *disappoint* you. When he says that God never has to *repent,* it's because God never changes His mind about the promises that He has made.

What It Means

God shielded the Israelites from harm when they didn't even know they needed protecting. He caused nations to be afraid of them and kept Israel from being cursed. God was so powerful that even Balaam had to say, "I have received a command to bless; He has blessed, and

I cannot reverse it" (Numbers 23:20). God's Word is absolutely true. You may not understand how God is going to bring about what He's promised, but He is keeping every promise that He has ever made. He will never deceive you, disappoint you, or change His mind about what He's told you.

The name *Balaam* means *not of the people.* Isn't it amazing that someone who had nothing to do with God's people could still recognize the faithfulness and power of God?

Life Examples

1. Read Exodus 19:5, Numbers 14:8–9, and Joshua 24:9–10. How did God fulfill His promise to protect the people of Israel from their enemies?

2. Read Isaiah 55:10–11. What do these verses say about God's promises?

3. How can this passage encourage you when your situation looks bleak?

4. Read Romans 15:4. What does this verse mean to you?

***

God's promises are essential to your spiritual welfare.

***

5. What Scripture passages or Bible stories most encourage you? Why?

Living the Principle

Do you meditate on the Bible every day so the Lord can bring His Word to your mind when you need a reminder of His love? What do you do when you're experiencing a tempest of adversity and need a special message of hope from God? When trouble strikes like a tidal wave, God's Word can be an anchor of strength, guidance, and comfort to keep you steady.

God will never fail you, and He'll never change His mind about the promises He's made to you. So lay your heart out to God and ask for His comfort. Ask Him to show you His will and lead you to His message of encouragement. Then read His wonderful Word. A good place to find assurance is the book of Psalms, or, if you are a new believer, read the gospel of John. Ask godly friends what Scripture passages have been meaningful and inspiring to them.

How will you live out Life Principle 3 this week? Think of ways you can keep God's Word as your anchor during difficult times. Also consider how the Bible has encouraged you and kept your focus on God in the past. Spend time in prayer, asking God to draw you into communion with Himself and to transform your life so you can affect the world for His kingdom.

Life Lessons to Remember

- ᴥ Consider God's promises your spiritual anchors (see Hebrews 6:18–20).
- ᴥ Remember God always keeps the promises that He makes (see Joshua 21:45).
- ᴥ Be willing to patiently wait for God to fulfill His promises (see Habakkuk 2:2–3).

LIFE PRINCIPLE 4

The Awareness of God's Presence Energizes You for Your Work

"When you go out to battle against your enemies . . . do not be afraid of them; for the LORD your God is with you."

DEUTERONOMY 20:1

Life's Questions

Ecclesiastes 2:24 teaches, "Nothing is better for a man than that . . . his soul should enjoy good in his labor." This may be a challenging verse for you, especially if you don't have a fulfilling profession. Maybe you're a caregiver to your children, spouse, or aging parents and you do an immense amount of work that is sometimes thankless and exhausting.

Even if you really like your job, you may not always find it enjoyable. Every occupation brings with it certain difficulties and frustrations. Likewise, you may not always recognize God's hand in what you are doing or appreciate the work deep down in your soul. You may feel like crying out, as Solomon himself once did, "Meaningless! Meaningless . . . Utterly meaningless! Everything is meaningless" (Ecclesiastes 1:2 NIV).

How do you feel about the work you do? Is it your dream job or just something that pays the bills? Whatever your situation may be, God expects you to do your best at whatever you do. Whether it's people, politics, or other kinds of problems that are causing you distress, you may wonder how you can stay motivated and honor God in your labors. Life Principle 4 gives you this encouragement: *The awareness of God's presence energizes you for your work.*

What the Bible Says

1. Read Deuteronomy 20:1–4. What kind of assignment did God guarantee that Israel would face (see verse 1)?

2. Why might the people of Israel have been terrified and discouraged (see verse 1)?

3. What did God promise that He would do for them (see verse 4)?

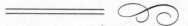

The word *afraid* in the Old Testament also means to *stand in awe of, revere,* or *respect.* Only God deserves your awe, respect, and reverence (see Deuteronomy 3:22). He is with you and is able to overcome anything that you'll ever face.

4. Read Deuteronomy 11:7–12. Why was it important for the people of Israel to stay focused on God during this crucial time in the nation's history (see verses 8–9)?

5. What did God reveal about the land they were about to enter (see verses 10–12)?

What It Means

The people of Israel were right: they could not conquer the Promised Land on their own. This is why they needed to look to God for courage when they faced challenges, enemies, or seemingly impossible situations. You may be wondering what this has to do with your job. As a believer, you're a servant of the living God every moment, with every task. Whether you're driving enemy armies out of the Promised Land, changing diapers, making multimillion dollar deals, delivering pizzas, or teaching a Sunday school class, you must honor God in all you do.

Life Examples

1. What is the worst job that you can think of? Why is it so terrible?

2. Read Genesis 39:20–23. What do you imagine Joseph's life was like in the prison?

3. Why did the keeper of the prison have such confidence in Joseph (see verses 22–23)?

───── ❦ ─────

Joseph spent at least a decade in that prison, but none of it was wasted time. God used that invaluable experience to teach him the principles that he would need when governing Egypt and to position him for maximum impact and blessings.

4. Read Genesis 41:15–16, 38–44. How did God bless Joseph for his faithfulness?

5. Read Genesis 41:53–57. What was the end result of Joseph's faithfulness?

Living the Principle

How can you stay motivated and honor God in your work? Joseph did it by remembering God was with him no matter what happened. He determined to serve God faithfully, whether in the prison or the palace, and regardless of famine or fruitfulness. The same should be true for you.

Like Joseph, you may not know why God has allowed the difficulties you face. It's possible you have a goal in mind with regard to your profession, but God's plan is much greater. Obey Him and don't lose heart (see Galatians 6:9). He is your energy, strength, wisdom, and creativity. He is also your boss. So do your best for His sake and allow Him to work through you. He's got a great victory and a wonderful reward for you if you'll trust Him and do as He says.

"My elect shall long enjoy the work of their hands.
They shall not labor in vain" (Isaiah 65:22–23).

How will you live out Life Principle 4 this week? Have you encountered a situation at work that causes you fear or discourages you? Consider how you can keep your mind focused on God's presence and honor Him in your work. Then spend some time in prayer, asking God to transform your life so that you can affect the world for the sake of His kingdom.

Life Lessons to Remember

- ❧ View yourself as a servant (see Philippians 2:5–7).
- ❧ Realize that you work for the Lord Himself (see Ephesians 2:10).
- ❧ Realize that your pay comes both now and hereafter (see 1 Corinthians 3:13–14).

LIFE PRINCIPLE 5

God Does Not Require You to Understand His Will, Just Obey It, Even If It Seems Unreasonable

"You shall command the priests who bear the ark of the covenant, saying, 'When you have come to the edge of the water of the Jordan, you shall stand in the Jordan.'"

JOSHUA 3:8

Life's Questions

Are things in your life not going the way you planned? Do you feel out of step with your heavenly Father? Is it difficult for you to understand what went wrong in a particular situation or why God doesn't seem to be blessing you? If so, it may be time for a careful self-evaluation.

Sometimes, it may feel as if God is no longer working in your life because you've insisted on doing things your way instead of His way. Perhaps you've placed a condition on God, and you'll only obey Him when you think His instructions are logical. What this really means is you've failed to commit yourself to Him completely and failed to trust in His will with your whole heart. This is bound to cause frustration in your life.

If it seems as if your prayers are going unanswered or that the path ahead is blocked, then it could be that God is waiting for you to take the step of faith that He's commanded. Don't lose hope about your circumstances. Instead, embrace Life Principle 5: *God does not require you to understand His will, just obey it, even if it seems unreasonable.*

What the Bible Says

1. Read Joshua 3. What were the people to look for when crossing the Jordan River (see verse 3)?

2. Why would the people have been fearful about crossing the Jordan (see verse 4)?

The Jordan River normally has many fording places, but this episode takes place during the grain harvest, when the spring rains and the melting snow from Mount Hermon would have flooded the Jordan's banks and made it completely impassable. Also, enemies and beasts such as vipers, scorpions, crocodiles, and lions could hide in the overgrown brush along the banks.

---

3. What was God's promise to the people if they obeyed Him (see verse 5)?

4. What was God going to teach the Israelites (see verses 7–11)?

5. What do you think would have happened if the Israelites had not obeyed God?

What It Means

Imagine you were planning to lead an enormous group of people across an overflowing river into enemy territory. It's likely the last thing you would want to do is send your most important people with your most valuable possession in first to test the waters—especially rushing floodwaters. Yet that is exactly what God sent Israel's priests to do at the Jordan River. God's command did not make sense to them, but He had another purpose in mind, which was to teach them to always keep their eyes on Him instead of their circumstances.

Life Examples

1. Read Joshua 6. What was God's command to the Israelites concerning the city of Jericho (see verses 2–6)?

2. What did God say would cause the walls of Jericho to fall (see verse 5)?

Archaeological discoveries have shown that Jericho's outer wall would have been approximately six feet thick, and the inner wall twelve feet thick.

---

3. What was similar about this event and the crossing of the Jordan (see verse 6)?

4. How closely did the people of Israel have to obey God (see verse 10)?

5. What was the result of the Israelites' obedience and God's
faithfulness (see verses 20, 27)?

Living the Principle

What has God called you to do? Do His instructions seem extreme
or confusing? Has He challenged you to do something that you don't
feel capable of doing? Remember, it is not your job to *understand* God's
plan but to *obey* Him. God sees the beginning, middle, and end of your
situation, so His perspective is far more complete than your own. If
you could just see things from His point of view, you would be highly
motivated to obey Him.

True obedience means doing what God says, when
He says it, how He says it should be done, until what
He says is accomplished—regardless of whether
you understand the reasons for it or not.

Unfortunately, if you disobey Him, you will continue to struggle
in the same area repeatedly, and you will lose out on His blessings.
God's goal is to grow your trust in Him, so He will give you assign-
ments that test your heart and mature your faith. The good news is
that when you submit to God, He shows you His faithfulness and
empowers you by His Holy Spirit to do everything that He calls you
to do. Your obedience—even though you don't understand what He is
doing—exercises your faith and makes it stronger.

How will you live out Life Principle 5 this week? Consider what seems
"illogical" about what God has commanded you to do. Why does His

direction intimidate you? How can you overcome these feelings and start to step forward in obedience and faith? Spend some time today in prayer, asking God to draw you into intimate communion with Himself and to transform your life so that you can affect the world for the sake of His kingdom.

Life Lessons to Remember

- ✣ Obedience must be the top priority of your life (see Psalm 119:145).
- ✣ The Holy Spirit enables you to walk obediently before God (see John 14:26).
- ✣ God produces good fruit in your life through your obedience to Him (see Jeremiah 29:11).

LIFE PRINCIPLE 6

You Reap What You Sow, More than You Sow, and Later than You Sow

"You have not obeyed My voice. Why have you done this? Therefore I also said . . . 'They shall be thorns in your side, and their gods shall be a snare to you.'"

JUDGES 2:2-3

Life's Questions

Picture a farmer at the start of the growing season, plowing his field to get it ready for that year's crops. Whatever seed the farmer plants is what the field will produce. If he plants tomato seeds, he will grow tomatoes. If he plants pumpkin seeds, he will grow pumpkins. He will always harvest the product of the kind of seed that he has planted.

The farmer will also take from the ground far more than he put into it. The tiny seed he plants in the spring will sprout and become a plant that produces fruit in the fall, which will then yield many more seeds. Of course, this is not an instantaneous process. The farmer must wait for the crop to mature in its time. He must be patient and care for the seeds he has planted. The rewards of the harvest always come later than the initial investment.

What seeds are you planting? What would you like to accomplish with your life? It's extremely important for you to be conscious of what you are sowing with your words and actions, because they set the direction of your life. This is why it's critical for you to embrace Life Principle 6: *You reap what you sow, more than you sow, and later than you sow.*

What the Bible Says

1. Read Deuteronomy 7:1–6. What was God's command to the Israelites (see verses 1–2)?

2. Why was the Lord so strict about this issue (see verse 4)?

―――― ∽◯∼ ――――

Idolatry in the Old Testament was often prompted by
legitimate needs. For example, the Canaanites worshiped
Ba'al, whom they believed to be the deity of storms and
fertility, in the hopes that he would provide rain for their
harvests. Unfortunately, the Israelites were also turning to
Ba'al out of the false belief that he would provide a better
yield for their harvests. They didn't have faith that God would
provide for their needs, even after all He had done for them.

3. What was the Lord's motivation in giving them this command
(see verse 6)?

4. Read Judges 1:27–34. Why do you think the Israelites ignored
God and failed to drive these foreign nations out?

5. Read Judges 2:1–4. What did the Israelites reap from their
disobedience (see verse 3)?

What It Means

Did the Israelites allow the other nations to stay because they thought they could profit from them? Was it because it was just too much effort to drive them out? Whatever the case, the people's disobedience to God brought them a great deal of trouble. They weren't judged immediately, yet the consequences came all the same. As we read in Judges, "When all that generation had been gathered to their fathers, another generation arose after them who did not know the LORD nor the work which He had done for Israel. Then the children of Israel did evil in the sight of the LORD, and served the Baals" (2:10–11). As a result of the Israelites' disobedience, they suffered hundreds of years of warfare with the nations that they failed to drive out.

It is dangerous to think that "God won't mind" when you disobey. He *does* mind. You may not immediately see the consequences of your actions, but they are coming.

Life Examples

1. Read Galatians 6:7–10. Why do you think Paul says, "God is not mocked" (verse 7) about the things that you reap and sow?

2. What actions or attitudes do you consider sowing in the flesh (see verse 8)?

3. What actions or attitudes do you consider sowing in the Spirit (see verse 8)?

This principle is not about doing "good works," it's about being obedient to God. Plenty of people do "good works" with selfish intentions, and Jesus says to them, "I never knew you; depart from Me, you who practice lawlessness!" (Matthew 7:23).

---

4. Why do good deeds and obedience take more effort than doing evil (see verse 9)?

5. What will you reap if you obey God and don't lose heart?

Living the Principle

Do you seek God's leadership when you make a decision? Do you obey Him as soon as you know His will? Each choice that you make for good or evil is a seed that you are planting for your future—and sometimes it will be the smallest decisions that will affect you the most.

This is because sin turns your heart away from God, while obedience turns your heart toward Him.

If you fill your life with God's Spirit and His Word, you will reap the fruit of the Spirit (see Galatians 5:22–23) and enjoy all that God created you to be. But if you're disobedient, greedy, and selfish, you're going to reap the terrible consequences of your ungodly lifestyle. So it's time to get serious about following God. You must decide what kind of life you are going to live and commit yourself to living it, because someday soon you'll see the return of what you've planted over the years. Will that be a crop that you're proud of producing?

How will you live out Life Principle 6 this week? Think about what God is calling you to sow with your life. Is there any area of your life where you are already seeing a harvest? Spend some time in prayer, asking God to draw you into intimate communion with Himself and to transform your life so that you can affect the world for the sake of His kingdom.

Life Lessons to Remember

- ❧ You will reap what you sow (see Luke 6:43–45).
- ❧ You will reap more than you sow (see John 12:23–25).
- ❧ You will reap later than you sow (see Isaiah 49:4; Mark 9:41).

LIFE PRINCIPLE 7

The Dark Moments of Your Life Will Last Only So Long as Is Necessary for God to Accomplish His Purpose in You

The soul of all the people was grieved, every man for his sons and his daughters. But David strengthened himself in the LORD his God.

1 SAMUEL 30:6

Life's Questions

Sometimes it can seem as if the trials in life will never really end. You're either beginning a season of difficulties, or you're in the middle of one, or you're just ending one. Whether the trial is relational, financial, physical, or spiritual, it can be extremely draining and discouraging. What's more, the problems don't happen in a vacuum—there are always new emergencies and troubles to deal with that make life even more difficult.

Yet the Bible says that God is *always* good. "The LORD [is] merciful and gracious, longsuffering, and abounding in goodness and truth" (Exodus 34:6). Of course, this can be a difficult truth to accept when you're going through a trial, because you only have a limited perspective on your dark moments. You can see how you are being affected in the moment, but you can't see the bigger picture of what God is accomplishing during those dark times.

If you want God's best for your life and desire to be used by Him, at some point you will travel the road of adversity. At those times, you will have to trust that God wants only what is ultimately best for you. It will also be helpful to remember Life Principle 7: *The dark moments of your life will last only so long as is necessary for God to accomplish His purpose in you.*

What the Bible Says

1. Read 1 Samuel 27:1–8. David had been anointed king of Israel by the prophet Samuel while the present king, a man named Saul, was still alive (see 1 Samuel 16:11–13). What is going on at this point in David's life (see verse 1)?

David didn't have it easy. In addition to waiting years
for God to give him the throne, King Saul wanted
to kill him and anyone else who helped him.

---

2. How long was David with the Philistines? Where did Achish, the king of the Philistines, tell David to dwell (see verses 5–7)?

3. Read 1 Samuel 29:3–7. How did the Philistines react to seeing David (see verse 4)? How do you think David felt to be unwanted in his homeland and rejected by the Philistines?

4. Read 1 Samuel 30:1–6. What did David and his men find when they got home to Ziklag (see verses 1–3)?

5. Who did all the people blame for their misfortunes (see verse 6)?

What It Means

You can't blame David for despairing, because everything was going wrong. He was unfairly targeted by Saul, driven from his homeland, rejected by his new neighbors, and constantly under threat of attack. His family was taken captive and his people were turning on him. If there was ever a moment for David to wonder what God was doing, this was it. Yet David did what we all should do when the dark moments of life overwhelm us: "David strengthened himself in the LORD his God" (1 Samuel 30:6). Instead of doubting God, David spent time in His presence, reminding himself of the mighty God that he trusted and served.

God chose David to be king of Israel years before David ever occupied the throne. God first had to prepare David to honor Him in everything that he did. There was *never* any question that God would keep His promise to David, no matter how David doubted or suffered. All of the trials merely strengthened David's faith for the challenges to come.

Life Examples

1. Read Isaiah 30:18–21. What does God want to do (see verse 18)?

2. When you cry out to God, how does He respond (see verse 19)?

3. Why does God allow adversity in your life (see verses 20–21)?

4. Read 1 Peter 1:6–9. Why can you rejoice even when you are facing dark times?

5. What are some trials you have been through lately? How have you seen God use those trials to build your faith in Him?

Living the Principle

Trials are confusing and are never easy. But God uses them to develop important character traits in your life, and you can profit from your troubles if you will trust Him. David did, and he passed the tests of faith (see 1 Samuel 31:6; 2 Samuel 2:4; 2 Samuel 5:1–5). God taught David through the affliction that he faced, and He is teaching you as well.

You may wonder why it has to be so painful. Unfortunately, there are no simple answers, because God's discipline and instruction are unique to each person. God must get your attention, teach you to turn only to Him, and train you to minister to others who have hurts (see 2 Corinthians 1:3–4)—and usually that requires touching an area deep within your soul. However, you can know for sure that He is doing something immensely important in and through you. God would never allow you to suffer without a significant reason or permit your trouble to continue a minute more than necessary. Therefore, don't run from your problems. Face them with faith in God, knowing that He will not give you more than you can bear.

How will you live out Life Principle 7 this week? Are you experiencing a dark and difficult time? Do you need the relief only God can give? Consider how to "strengthen yourself in the Lord" as David did. Spend time in prayer, asking God to draw you into communion with Himself and to transform your life so that you can affect the world for the sake of His kingdom.

Life Lessons to Remember

- God has put a limit on all adversity (see Lamentations 3:31–33).
- Adversity is God's tool for building godly character in us (see Romans 5:3–4).
- God's ultimate design is to conform you to the likeness of Jesus (see Romans 8:29).

LIFE PRINCIPLE 8

Fight All Your Battles on Your Knees and You Win Every Time

Someone told David, saying, "Ahithophel is among the
conspirators with Absalom." And David said, "O LORD, I
pray, turn the counsel of Ahithophel into foolishness!"
2 SAMUEL 15:31

Life's Questions

Have you ever been wrongly accused by someone? Have you ever endured the wrath and rejection of a loved one? Perhaps some of the most hurtful situations that you've experienced came through such condemnation. Whether or not you merited that person's criticism, the pain he or she inflicted was no doubt devastating and probably took a long time to overcome.

What is your first instinct when your heart is broken by another? Perhaps it is to confront the person, accuse him or her of wrongdoing, and then do everything in your power to make that person's life miserable. When faced with ongoing personal attacks, you may be tempted to "fight fire with fire," seek vengeance where you can find it, and give your attacker a taste of his or her own medicine. After all, it is just human nature.

Yet the Bible urges you to resist such gut reactions. As a child of God, you have a *responsibility* to respond in a godly manner when someone challenges you to combat—and that begins with going to God first. In this, you can see that Life Principle 8 holds the key to turning your circumstances around: *Fight all your battles on your knees and you win every time.*

What the Bible Says

1. Read 2 Samuel 13:1–14, 23–28. Who were Absalom, Tamar, and Amnon? What did Absalom do to avenge his sister Tamar (see verse 28)?

2. Read 2 Samuel 13:37–38. What was Absalom forced to do? What is your initial impression of Absalom's character after reading these verses?

3. Read 2 Samuel 15:1–12. Eventually, Absalom returned to Israel. Do Absalom's actions at this point confirm your initial impression of him? Why or why not?

Hebron was where David was anointed king of Israel (see 2 Samuel 5), and it was also where Abraham, Isaac, and Jacob were buried. It was a symbolic center of Israel's leadership, making it the perfect place for Absalom to stage his coup. With the murder of David's firstborn son Amnon, and the death of his second son Chileab (also called Daniel), Absalom was next in line for the throne and was ready to take it.

---

4. Do you think that Absalom's time away from Jerusalem healed the anger that he had toward Amnon? Why or why not?

5. Read 2 Samuel 15:13–16, 23–31. How do you think David felt when he found out his son had betrayed him? What was David most interested in finding out (see verses 25–26)?

Almost 1,000 years after David went to the Mount of Olives to seek God, his descendant, Jesus the Messiah, went there as well. At the foot of the Mount of Olives is the garden of Gethsemane, where Jesus accepted the Father's will (see Luke 22:42) and prepared to do battle with our sin on the cross.

What It Means

Can you imagine how devastating it was for King David to be betrayed by his son? In every way, this was a lose-lose situation. David could not regain his kingdom without hurting his son and many of his countrymen, and he couldn't restore his relationship with his son while the kingdom hung in the balance. No slingshot or sword would solve his problem—but God could.

Life Examples

1. Read Psalm 3. When have you felt as David did in verses 1–2?

David wrote Psalm 3 while he was fleeing from Absalom.

2. Why was it important for David to know the Lord was his shield (see verse 3)?

3. What would you say David's mood was in the midst of this terrible trial (see verses 5–6)?

4. How do you feel knowing that your vindication comes from God (see verses 7–8)?

5. Does this encourage you, or do you feel cheated that you cannot take revenge? Explain.

Living the Principle

When David fled from Absalom, the situation seemed dire. Absalom had gained popularity among the people, and it appeared the nation was with him. But it wasn't long after that God delivered the kingdom of Israel back into David's hands. Although David did everything he could to protect his son, Absalom still lost his life (see 2 Samuel 18).

This is what always happens when people harbor unforgiveness and revenge in their heart. They hurt the people around them unnecessarily and eventually destroy themselves. This is why, when people attack you, you can't react out of fear and rage. You must be like David and have a battle plan. Your combat strategy must begin and end with getting on your knees and realizing God is in control of your situation. He will handle everything for you if you will humble yourself and obey Him. However, you must stop being distracted by your own feelings and circumstances and put your focus on Him. Whenever you surrender yourself completely to God and trust Him with your struggles, you'll find that He is faithful to lead you to victory.

How will you live out Life Principle 8 this week? Are you facing a battle that seems like a lose-lose situation? Are you heartbroken by someone's accusations? Consider your battle plan for taking your trouble to God and surrendering yourself to Him. Then spend some time in prayer, asking God to draw you into intimate communion with Himself and to transform your life so that you can affect the world for the sake of His kingdom.

Life Lessons to Remember

- ❧ Prayer and obedience to God are the biblical approach to overcoming all of your troubles (see 2 Chronicles 7:14; Philippians 4:6–7).
- ❧ You can remain firm in your faith only when you completely submit all areas of your life to God (see James 4:7–10).
- ❧ Having a prayer-centered battle plan in place will help you respond effectively when troubling circumstances arise (see Luke 18:1–8).

LIFE PRINCIPLE 9

Trusting God Means Looking Beyond What You Can See to What God Sees

Elisha prayed, and said, "Lord, I pray, open his eyes that he may see." Then the Lord opened the eyes of the young man, and he saw.

2 KINGS 6:17

Life's Questions

You don't know what tomorrow may bring. This truth may cause you some anxiety, but when your faith is in God, it *should* bring you hope. God sees tomorrow—*all* of your tomorrows—and He is able to prepare you for whatever is to come. So, what is it about the future that causes you to be afraid? Is it a conflict that you dread? Are you doubtful about ever receiving your heart's desire? Are you caught in a bad situation that you fear will never change?

The Bible is clear that you are not to give in to fear and anxiety. Jesus commanded, "Let not your heart be troubled, neither let it be afraid" (John 14:27). But when you are facing the uncertainties of life, this can be difficult to do. Yet it is those times when God's command is the most pertinent: Do *not* be afraid! The Lord provides you with all the resources you need to overcome fear. Your part is to trust that God sees more than your limited perspective and be confident that He is working in ways you cannot see.

The circumstances in your life may be truly overwhelming, but God's resources are even greater and more powerful than you can imagine. God knows what is ahead—and He is ready to deal with it. Therefore, put your faith in Him and obey whatever He says. As Life Principle 9 teaches: *Trusting God means looking beyond what you can see to what God sees.*

What the Bible Says

1. Read 2 Kings 6:8–23. How did Elisha know where the Syrians were going to ambush the Israelites (see verses 9–12)?

Elisha's mentor, Elijah, was taken up to heaven in a chariot of fire. Before he departed, Elisha asked him for a double portion of his spirit (see 2 Kings 2:9–11).

2. How did the king of Syria respond when Elisha learned his secret plans? How would you have reacted if you were Elisha's servant (see verses 12–15)?

3. Do you think Elisha was surprised by the Syrian army? Why or why not?

4. Why do you think Elisha could see the Lord's forces but the servant could not (see verses 16–17)?

5. The Syrian army started out hunting Elisha and ended up following him to Samaria. Why do you think they agreed to follow him (see verses 19–20)?

We think of Jerusalem as the capital of Israel, but after Solomon's reign in 922 BC, the nation was divided into two kingdoms: Israel and Judah. Jerusalem remained the capital of Judah, while Samaria became the capital of Israel. Elisha led the Syrian army twelve miles from Dothan into the heart of Israel.

What It Means

When you judge a situation by your limited perspective, it means that you aren't getting the whole picture. Elisha understood this, which is why he was so eager to hear whatever God had to say to him. He determined to look beyond what he could see to the Lord's reality—and when he did, "behold, the mountain was full of horses and chariots of fire" (2 Kings 6:17). God showed Elisha some amazing things and did some awesome miracles through him.

Life Examples

1. Read 1 Corinthians 2:9–16. Why does Paul include eyes, ears, and hearts in verse 9? What does this suggest about God's perspective and your perspective?

2. What is the only way that we can know what God is doing in our lives (see verse 10)?

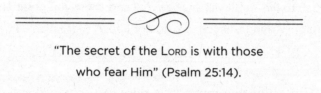

"The secret of the LORD is with those
who fear Him" (Psalm 25:14).

3. Why does God communicate to us through the Spirit (see verses 11–13)?

4. What will worldly people think when they hear God's plans (see verse 14)? Why?

5. Why should God's plans make sense to you if you've accepted Christ as your Savior (see verses 15–16)?

Living the Principle

How did Elisha know the Syrians' plans and that the Lord's army was protecting him? He listened to the Spirit of God. You may think it is difficult to pay attention to God when you face overwhelming troubles, especially those that seem impossible. Like Elisha's servant, your mind searches for a way to deal with what you're seeing. In despair you cry out, "What can I do?"

———— ⚬⚬ ————

"Call to Me, and I will answer you, and show you great and mighty things, which you do not know" (Jeremiah 33:3).

————————

The first thing you must do is close your physical eyes, because they're not helping. Stop measuring your problems against your ability to handle them, because the enemy will use your worldly senses to magnify your situation. You must then open your spiritual eyes—the ones fixed on God. Worship Him. Read His Word. Pray. Remember how He has helped others in the past and thank Him that the mighty wisdom and power that was available to them has been provided to you as well. God is ready, willing, and able to rescue you from the jaws of defeat, and He will do whatever is necessary to lead you to triumph when you obey Him.

How will you live out Life Principle 9 this week? Think about how you can better focus your mind and heart on God's truth rather than on what you can see. Then spend some time in prayer, asking God to draw you into intimate communion with Himself and to transform your life so that you can affect the world for the sake of His kingdom.

Life Lessons to Remember

- Recall past victories (see Psalm 145:5–7).
- Recognize the true nature of the battle (see Psalm 20:6–8).
- Rely on the power of God (see Psalm 66:3–5).

LIFE PRINCIPLE 10

If Necessary, God Will
Move Heaven and Earth
to Show You His Will

"O our God . . . we have no power against this great
multitude that is coming against us; nor do we know
what to do, but our eyes are upon You."
2 CHRONICLES 20:12

Life's Questions

What is God's will for your life? Do you have an answer, or do you think, *Good question!* Perhaps you know how God is leading you in certain areas, and you're committed to following Him. However, there are other situations that you are facing in which you have no idea about what to do, and you wish that God would show you the right course of action. You wonder, *Why does God's will seem hidden from me? Can I truly know what God has planned for my life?*

Yes you can! God does not hide His will from you. As Paul writes, He wants to make the riches of His grace abound to you "in all wisdom and prudence" (Ephesians 1:8). He has made known to you "the mystery of His will" and given you "the spirit of wisdom and revelation in the knowledge of Him" (9, 17). The Lord has provided everything necessary through His indwelling Spirit so you can know Him profoundly, understand His ways, and see the path He purposes for you.

In the midst of all the confusing and overwhelming details in your world today, God takes the lead in teaching you the way to go. He is committed to showing you how to follow the plan He has designed for your life. As He does, you will come to understand the truth of Life Principle 10: *If necessary, God will move heaven and earth to show you His will.*

What the Bible Says

1. Read 1 Kings 16:30–33. What kind of man was Ahab, the king of Israel?

Ahab was the seventh king of Israel. Through his wife, Jezebel,
he brought the Phoenician religion to Israel. He set the deities
of Tyre—Ba'al and Asherah—as equal with the Lord God and
allowed Jezebel to kill the prophets and priests of God.

---

2. Read 2 Chronicles 17:3–4 and 18:1–3. Considering Jehoshaphat's values, do you think it was wise for him to ally himself with Ahab? Why do you think he did so?

3. Read 2 Chronicles 18:28–34. How did God show Jehoshaphat that an alliance with Ahab was *not* His will (see verses 31–34)?

4. Read 2 Chronicles 19:1–3. How did God confirm that Jehoshaphat had done the wrong thing?

5. What had Jehoshaphat done that was pleasing to God? What idols need to be removed in your own life?

What It Means

We do not know why Jehoshaphat decided to ally himself with Ahab. It could be that he saw an opportunity to reunite the kingdoms of Israel and Judah as they had been under David. It could also be that he thought an alliance with Israel would strengthen his military position or increase his wealth. Whatever the case, he failed to seek God in the matter and depend on Him for everything—and that decision nearly cost him his life.

Life Examples

1. Read 2 Chronicles 20:1-30. What terrible threat was Judah now facing (see verses 1-2)? How did Jehoshaphat react to the crisis?

2. What was God's message to Jehoshaphat (see verse 15)?

3. Why do you think God refused to allow Jehoshaphat to participate in the battle?

4. God's instruction to Jehoshaphat required a great test of faith. Do you think Jehoshaphat had learned his lesson about trusting God (see verse 18)?

5. What did Jehoshaphat instruct the people of Judah to do when God delivered the victory to Judah (see verses 20–22)? What is the connection?

"You are holy, enthroned in the praises of Israel.
Our fathers trusted in You; they trusted, and
You delivered them" (Psalm 22:3–4).

Living the Principle

God's will is *His* to communicate and fulfill. No matter what God reveals to be His plan, He will make sure everything is in place for it to come to pass. Your responsibility is simply to obey Him *right now*. It is God's right to exclude or include you from the battle as He so desires.

God knows precisely what it will take to get your attention.

If you feel that God's will remains a mystery to you, perhaps it is because He is revealing it one step at a time. God knows every detail of your circumstances and how they will unfold, but He does not always reveal them all at once. Instead, He may use the situation as an opportunity to teach you to trust Him. If you are unwilling to wait for His timing, you are going to prolong your struggle and miss maturing in your faith.

Another reason why it may seem that God's will is hidden is because you've failed to obey Him in some capacity. Understand that you will not move forward until you submit to Him in every area. Just like Jehoshaphat, you must surrender yourself to God completely, whether it means engaging in the battle under God's leadership or watching what He is doing from the sidelines.

How will you live out Life Principle 10 this week? Are you having trouble discerning God's will? Consider how God may be trying to get your attention, whether through your restless spirit, an unusual blessing, unanswered prayer, disappointment, financial trouble, or affliction. Then spend some time in prayer, asking God to draw you into intimate communion with Himself and to transform your life so that you can affect the world for the sake of His kingdom.

Life Lessons to Remember

- ❧ God always knows exactly where you are in your journey of faith (see Romans 8:29–30).
- ❧ God is committed to helping you live out the specific plan that He has designed for you (see Jeremiah 29:11–13).
- ❧ The key to understanding God's will is to listen to Him (see Isaiah 30:19–21).

LIFE PRINCIPLE 11

God Assumes Full Responsibility for Your Needs When You Obey Him

Now the LORD *blessed the latter days of Job more than his beginning.*
JOB 42:12

Life's Questions

It's in times of great loss or trial that you may be tempted to question whether God really cares about you. If certain things have gone terribly wrong, and you find there are needs in your life that continue to go unmet, it can strike an unpleasant chord deep inside you. You may find yourself wrestling with thoughts of doubt or uncertainty.

You believe that the Lord is God—the all-powerful Creator and Sustainer of the universe. Everything you know about Him confirms that He is fully capable of providing for you. You've seen Him take care of others. You've read passages of Scripture that teach He helps those in need. So the questions arise: *Why isn't God delivering me? Why has He allowed these bad things to happen? Haven't I been faithful? Does He really want to help me?*

Yes, He does. God takes great joy in meeting your needs and supplying the desires of your heart. Yet there is a condition: complete submission and dependence on Him. Is obeying God the top priority in your life? Are you submitting fully to Him? Are you trusting in Him? As Life Principle 11 states, *God assumes full responsibility for your needs when you obey Him.*

What the Bible Says

1. Read Job 1:1-3 and 6-12. What was Satan implying about why Job served God? Why do you think God allowed Satan to test Job (see verses 8-12)?

2. Read Job 1:13-22. What do you think about Job's response to his adversity (see verses 20-21)?

3. Read Job 2:1-10. Why do you think Job was able to remain so strong in the midst of such terrible pain and loss (see verse 10)?

"The LORD gave, and the LORD has taken away;
blessed be the name of the LORD" (Job 1:21).

4. Read Job 42:1–17. What need did God fill for Job that was not fulfilled by all the things that he had lost (see verse 5)?

"Though He slay me, yet will I trust Him" (Job 13:15).

5. Why did Job need to lose so much before he came to this profound understanding of God? Why do you think God gave him *twice* as much as he had before (see verses 10, 12)?

What It Means

Job obeyed God, but bad things still happened to him. Why? Was it merely to prove something to Satan, or was there a deeper reason? God was meeting more important needs in Job than we may initially realize. Remember Life Principle 1: *Your intimacy with God—His highest priority for your life—determines the impact of your life.* God took full responsibility for bringing Job into the deepest intimacy possible with Himself. And because of Job's obedience, people throughout the ages have been encouraged by his faithful example.

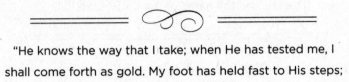

"He knows the way that I take; when He has tested me, I shall come forth as gold. My foot has held fast to His steps; I have kept His way and not turned aside" (Job 23:10–11).

Life Examples

1. What do you think you would have done if you had been in Job's shoes? Do you think your faith would have withstood all of those trials? Explain.

2. Read Luke 11:9–13. What is God's promise to you (see verses 9–10)?

3. What can you expect from God (see verses 11–12)?

4. Why can you count on God to give His very best for you (see verse 13)?

5. How would you describe your level of faith in God to meet your needs? What encouragement do you receive from this passage?

Living the Principle

Trusting in God requires you to settle two questions in your heart. First, *can* God help you? Do you believe that God is completely *able* to intervene in your situation? Do you have confidence in the One who laid the foundations of the earth (see Genesis 1), who delivered the children of Israel out of Egypt and parted the Red Sea (see Exodus 14:13–31), and who defeated death to save you from your sins and provide a home for you in heaven (see 1 Corinthians 15)?

Second, *will* God help you? Paul answers that question for you: "He who did not spare His own Son, but delivered Him up for us all, how shall He not with Him also freely give us all things?" (Romans 8:32). God is both able and willing to supply *everything* that you need. Therefore, if there are still areas in your life where you are lacking, spend time in prayer asking God to reveal what He is trying to teach you. Maybe there is something in your life that shouldn't be there, or perhaps He is filling a deeper need in you as He did with Job.

⎯⎯⎯⎯⎯⎯ ∽ ⎯⎯⎯⎯⎯⎯

"My God shall supply all your need according to His
riches in glory by Christ Jesus" (Philippians 4:19).

⎯⎯⎯⎯⎯⎯⎯⎯⎯⎯⎯⎯⎯

How will you live out Life Principle 11 this week? Is there something
that you need God to provide? Is God trying to reveal something special to you? Think about ways that you can stay faithful to God as Job
did, even when you don't understand what is going on. Then spend
some time in prayer, asking God to draw you into intimate communion with Himself and to transform your life so that you can affect the
world for the sake of His kingdom.

Life Lessons to Remember

- ❧ God is able to provide for you (see Psalm 65:4–6).
- ❧ God's integrity and love ensure that He will carry out His
  promises (see Psalm 37:25–28).
- ❧ God will work through you to meet the needs of others in this
  world (see Hebrews 13:16).

LIFE PRINCIPLE 12

Peace with God Is the Fruit of Oneness with God

I will both lie down in peace, and sleep; for You alone, O Lord, make me dwell in safety.

PSALM 4:8

Life's Questions

At night when everything is quiet, uneasy thoughts can bombard you. You want to sleep and get the rest you need, but your responsibilities and problems fill your mind. You try to focus on other things—counting sheep or the tick-tocks of your clock—but you can't stop the anxieties from tormenting you and keeping you awake. In those moments, you would give *anything* for some genuine, soul-calming peace.

Have you experienced sleepless nights alone with your troubled thoughts? Have you replayed scenarios over and over in your mind that you wish you could forget? Have you struggled through those stressful moments, wondering why your mind cannot let go and rest? You know in your heart that Jesus promised, "My peace I give to you; not as the world gives do I give to you. Let not your heart be troubled, neither let it be afraid" (John 14:27).

So, why is that peace so hard to grasp? Why does it seem so elusive? In truth, peace is God's gift to you, but you cannot have it apart from having a close, intimate relationship with Him. As Life Principle 12 states: *Peace with God is the fruit of oneness with God.*

What the Bible Says

1. Read 2 Samuel 19:9–15 and 40–43. Why were the people of Israel protesting?

When the Israelites spoke of their "ten shares in the king" (2 Samuel 19:43), they were referring to ten tribes. There were twelve tribes of Israel in total, but the tribe of Simeon was within the borders of Judah (see Joshua 19:1) and was considered part of Judah.

2. Read 2 Samuel 20:1-7. How widespread was Sheba's rebellion? How serious did David consider this rebellion to be (see verses 2, 6)?

3. Read 2 Samuel 20:15–22. How did God turn Sheba's rebellion around to restore the peace of Israel?

4. Read Psalm 4. Why was it important for David to remember that God had relieved him of his distress in the past (see verses 1, 3)?

Some scholars believe that Psalm 4 was written either during the rebellion of Sheba or while Saul was persecuting David. Others believe that Psalm 4, like Psalm 3, was written by David during Absalom's rebellion against him. No matter who sought to hurt him, David trusted in God for his peace.

5. What can you learn about David's relationship with God (see verses 7–8)? Why did David's relationship with God give him peace?

The word for peace in Hebrew, *shalom*, means the *completion, fulfillment, unity,* and *harmony* that come as a result of God's presence.

What It Means

Considering that David had so many enemies, it is difficult to imagine him getting a good night's sleep. However, David knew that he could rely on God for his safety and peace. This was the result of his faithful walk with the Lord. David was committed to obeying God and keeping his focus continually on Him. Because of that, David had peace—even in the worst situations.

Life Examples

1. Read Isaiah 26:3–4. When have you spent an extended period of time in prayer and worship, meditating on God's Word and enjoying His presence?

2. Did your time with God fill you with peace? Why or why not?

3. Why would keeping your focus on God fill you with peace?

4. Read Matthew 5:9. What does it mean to be a peacemaker? Why do you think that Jesus says such individuals are blessed?

5. How do you keep God's peace as a fixture in your life? How do you use it to continually guard your heart and mind?

Living the Principle

Do you long for deep and abiding peace? Does your soul need rest from the worries and stresses that surround you? Your anxiety is a telltale sign that your focus isn't where it should be. Instead of rejoicing in the strength, wisdom, and love of God, you have allowed your attention to be consumed by the details of your circumstances. You are so busy trying to figure out how to fix your situation that you've forgotten that the only effective solution is to submit to God. As Jesus said, "I have spoken to you, that in Me you may have peace. In the world you will have tribulation; but be of good cheer, I have overcome the world" (John 16:33).

It is time to start thinking differently about your situation. As Paul instructs in Romans 12:2, it is time to "be transformed by the renewing of your mind." You do this by continually filling your mind with the things of God—by beginning each day connecting with Him through prayer and reading His Word. Your time with God will give you the direction, strength, and focus you need and will fill you with the peace for which your heart yearns.

The word for *peace* in Greek, *eirene*, means *to bind together*. It is the harmony, security, and joy that come from a relationship with Jesus Christ.

How will you live out Life Principle 12 this week? Think about the trials you are currently facing in your life and how you can develop your "oneness" with Christ. Then spend some time in prayer, asking God to draw you into intimate communion with Himself and to transform your life so that you can affect the world for the sake of His kingdom.

Life Lessons to Remember

- Only God is equipped to handle our problems (see Psalm 62:5–7).
- Accepting God's timetable and instruction helps to dispel rising anxiety (see Habakkuk 2:1–3).
- The safest place for you when trials come is in the everlasting arms of Jesus (see Deuteronomy 33:27).

LIFE PRINCIPLE 13

Listening to God Is Essential to Walking with God

"Hear, O My people, and I will admonish you!
O Israel, if you will listen to Me!"
PSALM 81:8

Life's Questions

Have you ever been in a situation in which people simply refused to listen to you even though you had expertise in what was being discussed? Perhaps the solution to a problem seemed obvious to you, but others were so busy voicing their opinions that you couldn't get a word in edgewise. You tried to reason with them, but they refused to pay attention.

Frustrating, wasn't it? Now imagine what it must be like to be God in heaven, who possesses the most profound and complete knowledge about every topic in the universe. He has the wisdom that we need to solve all our problems—even the deepest ones. He is willing and available to assist us with all the resources that only He can provide. But unfortunately, whenever we bow our heads in prayer to communicate with Him, we do all the talking.

Is that what you do? Have you been one-sided in your conversations with God, telling Him your needs instead of listening to His instructions? As Life Principle 13 states, *Listening to God is essential to walking with God.* If you want to have a relationship with Him, you have to listen to Him. If you want God to transform your life, you need to hear what He's saying.

What the Bible Says

1. Read Psalm 81. Why was it important for the Israelites to remember all the good things that God had done for them on the New Moon, Sabbath, and other feast days (see verses 1–7; see also Deuteronomy 4:7–10)?

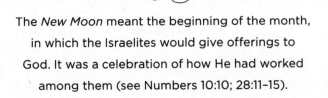

The *New Moon* meant the beginning of the month, in which the Israelites would give offerings to God. It was a celebration of how He had worked among them (see Numbers 10:10; 28:11–15).

2. How does recalling God's past provision help you when you pray?

3. What did God want from Israel? In what ways was He being gracious in His commands (see verses 8–10, 13–16)?

4. How did Israel respond to God (see verses 11–12)?

5. Why do you think Israel refused to listen to the Lord? Do you fail to listen to Him for similar reasons? Explain.

What It Means

God wants the best for His children, and He knows how to provide it. Unfortunately, the Israelites did not trust Him enough to embrace what He was teaching, and time after time they experienced the terrible consequences of their disobedience. They refused to listen to God, thinking that by doing so they were escaping His control. However, what they were really doing was rejecting His protection and love. Don't make the same mistake. God's commands are for your benefit. As we read in Proverbs 1:7, 33, "The fear of the LORD is the beginning of knowledge. . . . Whoever listens to me will dwell safely, and will be secure, without fear of evil."

Life Examples

1. Read Ecclesiastes 5:1–3. What attitude should you have when you go to God in prayer?

2. Read Matthew 6:5–8. What does Jesus mean when He says that the hypocrites have their reward (see verse 5)?

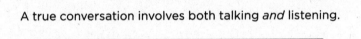

A true conversation involves both talking *and* listening.

3. Why is your prayer to be in secret, but God's reward is out in the open (see verse 6)?

4. What does Jesus say about the use of many words in prayer (see verse 7)?

5. If God already "knows the things you have need of before you ask Him" (verse 8), then why should you go before Him in prayer?

Living the Principle

Do you realize the amazing privilege you have in being able to go to God in prayer? You have the freedom to approach the God of all creation at any moment to ask for His wisdom, comfort, and power. "We do not have a High Priest who cannot sympathize with our weaknesses, but was in all points tempted as we are, yet without sin. Let us therefore come boldly to the throne of grace, that we may obtain mercy and find grace to help in time of need" (Hebrews 4:15–16).

Jesus understands everything that you're going through and all that you feel, and His desire is to guide you through your troubles in a way that glorifies God and makes you into an effective and mature believer. However, He cannot help you if you will not walk with Him, and you cannot walk with Him if you won't allow Him to lead you. And unfortunately, He cannot lead you if you refuse to listen to Him and obey His instructions.

Why should you listen to God? Because He always knows what is best for you.

How will you live out Life Principle 13 this week? Are you willing to be quiet before the Lord and hear what He has to say? Create an action plan of how you will intentionally listen to God and commit yourself to obeying Him, no matter what He tells you to do. Then spend some time in prayer, asking God to draw you into intimate communion with Himself and to transform your life so that you can affect the world for the sake of His kingdom.

Life Lessons to Remember

- God speaks in many ways, but you have to be willing to listen (see Hebrews 1:1–3).
- God always gives instruction for your benefit (see Isaiah 51:1–16).
- The choice is yours when it comes to obeying God's voice or the lies of the enemy (see Joshua 24:15).

LIFE PRINCIPLE 14

God Acts on Behalf of Those Who Wait for Him

For since the beginning of the world men have not heard
nor perceived by the ear, nor has the eye seen any God
besides You, who acts for the one who waits for Him.

ISAIAH 64:4

Life's Questions

Waiting is not fun. Perhaps you have been in the situation where you wake up hoping for some tidbit of good news, but it doesn't come, or you receive a negative report, and you see longer delays ahead. It can be frustrating. No wonder Proverbs 13:12 tells us, "Hope deferred makes the heart sick." The longer you wait to see your desire fulfilled, the more discouraged your heart grows. That is, of course, unless your hope and trust are centered exclusively on Christ.

In Micah 7:7, the prophet writes, "I will look to the LORD; I will wait for the God of my salvation; my God will hear me." Waiting is actually a big part of your walk of faith. God will use times of delay to refocus your attitude, remove hindrances that keep His will from being enacted, and prepare the way for you to take the next step in His plan. When you demonstrate your faith in His timetable, you acknowledge that He is Lord of your life.

One of the most difficult lessons that you will learn is to wait on God. However, it is crucial that you understand how truly important waiting on Him is. His knowledge of your situation is perfect—and so is His timing. He is going to make sure you are completely prepared for the blessings that He has for you. Therefore, make sure to keep your eyes on Him as you embrace Life Principle 14: *God acts on behalf of those who wait for Him.*

What the Bible Says

1. Read Isaiah 63:7–14. How does Isaiah describe God (see verses 7–9)?

2. How did the people respond to God's kindness? Why does God discipline His people (see verse 10; see also Hebrews 12:5–11)?

3. What did the people do after God disciplined them (see verses 11–13)?

<hr>

Isaiah ministered to Judah from 740 BC to 681 BC, and he prophesied about the Babylonian captivity that would begin a century later in 597 BC. The Babylonians would also destroy the temple in Jerusalem (see Isaiah 63:18) in 586 BC. In Isaiah 63:7–64:12, the prophet thanks God for His mercy in delivering His people from the Babylonian captivity.

<hr>

4. Read Isaiah 63:15–19. How did the people of Judah feel as they were held captive in Babylon? When have you felt this way?

5. Read Isaiah 64:1–4. What did Isaiah ask God to do (see verses 1–3)? What other hope was there for the people (see verse 4)?

What It Means

God was preparing His judgment for the kingdom of Judah, but He was also arranging for the deliverance of those who remained obedient to Him. Their only hope was to wait on Him for rescue. Thankfully, it was a sure hope, and God was faithful to bring them back to Jerusalem when the time was right and their hearts had turned back to Him. As God promises in Isaiah 49:23, "You will know that I am the Lord; those who hope in me will not be disappointed"(NIV).

Life Examples

1. Read Isaiah 40:27–31. What are you waiting for right now in your life?

2. Do you ever feel that your situation is "hidden from the Lord" (see verse 27)? Explain.

3. What does God do for you as you wait (see verse 29)?

───────── ❧ ─────────

When you wait for the Lord, you should look forward to what He will do with joyful expectation and confident hope, because He is providing His very best for you.

4. God understands how difficult the delays are for you (see verse 30). How does this encourage you?

5. What promise does God make if you commit yourself to waiting for Him (see verse 31)?

Living the Principle

During your season of waiting, you may feel lost, discouraged, and unmotivated. You may feel as if God has forgotten you. But know that He has not. God is always at work, and at this very moment He is engineering your situation to provide His best for you. In fact, He is lining up your circumstances in a way that is better than you could ever imagine (see Ephesians 3:20–21), and you are going to be completely blessed when you see what He has done for you.

However, you must be patient until His plan comes together. Do not run ahead of God! The delays may be challenging for you, but they are growing your faith in Him. After all, "Faith is the substance of things hoped for, the evidence of things not seen" (Hebrews 11:1). So look to Him, strengthen yourself in His Word and love, and remain confident that He is working on your behalf. Also, keep active as you wait. Waiting on God doesn't mean sitting around doing nothing but continuing in your present position until He gives you further instructions. As long as you are obeying Him, you will continue on the correct course.

"My soul, wait silently for God alone, for my expectation
is from Him. He only is my rock and my salvation; He
is my defense; I shall not be moved. . . . Trust in Him
at all times, you people; pour out your heart before
Him; God is a refuge for us" (Psalm 62:5–6, 8).

How will you live out Life Principle 14 this week? Think about the times
that you've waited for God to work and how He has acted on your
behalf. Then spend some time in prayer, asking God to draw you into
intimate communion with Himself and to transform your life so you
can affect the world for the sake of His kingdom.

Life Lessons to Remember

- When you wait, you discover God's will in the areas that most
  concern you (see Isaiah 30:18).
- When you wait, you receive supernatural physical energy and
  strength (see Psalm 27:13–14).
- When you wait, you see God working on your behalf (see
  Psalm 40:1–3).

LIFE PRINCIPLE 15

Brokenness Is God's Requirement for Maximum Usefulness

"If you return, then I will bring you back; you shall stand before Me;
if you take out the precious from the vile, you shall be as My mouth."
JEREMIAH 15:19

Life's Questions

Sometimes life just doesn't make sense. You seek God and try to be obedient to Him, but trouble and heartbreak confront you at every turn. Perhaps you thought that life would get easier after you accepted Christ as your Savior, but you've found just the opposite to be true. Now you not only have to deal with all the troubles the world throws at you, but you also feel responsible to honor God in how you respond to them.

Somewhere inside of you, you've come to the realization that you're just not strong enough to live the holy life that Christ has called you to. Good! God never meant you to live the Christian life by your own resources. The trials that you've been experiencing are part of the breaking process by which God frees you from your self-sufficiency so that you'll allow Christ to live in and through you. He wants to use the adversity you are facing as part of His miracle-working plan to mold you into the person He wants you to be.

It's through brokenness that God teaches you to stop depending on yourself, start looking to Him for wisdom and strength, and discover what He has planned for you. It's through brokenness that you become whole. This is why Life Principle 15 teaches, *Brokenness is God's requirement for maximum usefulness.*

What the Bible Says

1. Read 2 Kings 21:1–16. How did Manasseh's sin affect Judah (see verses 9–12, 16)?

2. Read Jeremiah 15:4–6. What was God's judgment on Judah?

Jeremiah was a prophet in Judah from c. 627 BC to 586 BC. He served *after* Manasseh's reign (c. 685 BC to 630 BC), but the ongoing corruption of the king's idolatry was felt throughout Judah for many years (see Exodus 20:4–5; Jeremiah 15:4). God's punishment for Judah was the Babylonian captivity. Jeremiah's sad duty was to warn the people of the judgment that was coming.

---

3. Read Jeremiah 15:15–21. How did Jeremiah respond to God's verdict (see verse 15)?

4. What was Jeremiah's concern about God's judgment? What was God's promise to Jeremiah (see verses 18–21)?

5. How do you think God would make Jeremiah into "a fortified bronze wall" (see verse 20; see also Jeremiah 1:18–19)?

Nothing could prevent God's judgment, yet Jeremiah
was still responsible to proclaim the truth to those
who were perishing, in the hope that they would
repent and be saved (see Jeremiah 18:8).

What It Means

Jeremiah was a godly man who had to endure the consequences of Manasseh's sin, even though he had nothing to do with the king's wickedness. God used the pressure to make Jeremiah into His holy mouthpiece—and his words have since brought hope to countless people undergoing similar persecution. Even when the adversity you are experiencing appears to be senseless, you can know that God allowed that trial for an eternal reason—a purpose beyond what you can see at the moment. You can be *absolutely* confident that God will use it for good in your life if you submit yourself to Him and trust Him (see 1 Peter 2:19–20).

Life Examples

1. Read 2 Corinthians 1:3–11. How does Paul describe God in verse 3?

2. How does God treat you while you are going through adversity (see verse 4)?

3. What is God training you to do as He is comforting you (see verses 4–5)?

4. Why would adversity make you a more effective minister of the gospel (see verse 6)?

5. What did Paul see as the purpose for his great suffering (see verses 8–10)?

Living the Principle

Romans 8:20–21 explains, "The creation was subjected to futility, not willingly, but because of Him who subjected it in hope; because the creation itself also will be delivered from the bondage of corruption into the glorious liberty of the children of God." In other words, you experience frustrating trials so that you can be free of the sin nature that is left within you. Yes, you are forgiven of *all* your sin when you accept Christ as your Lord and Savior. However, the tendency to *want* to sin remains within you, and He must break you of it.

God uses trials for two reasons: to transform you into the image of Christ (see Romans 8:29; Ephesians 5:1), and to develop your potential as His representative in the world (see Philippians 3:9–10; Colossians 1:24; Hebrews 2:18; 1 Peter 4:12–16). Therefore, commit yourself to God and heed the words of 1 Peter 4:19: "Those who suffer according to God's will should commit themselves to their faithful Creator and continue to do good" (NIV).

"In bringing many sons and daughters to glory, it was fitting that God, for whom and through whom everything exists, should make the pioneer of their salvation perfect through what he suffered" (Hebrews 2:10 NIV).

How will you live out Life Principle 15 this week? Consider the trials that you are facing in your life today and how you can remain faithful and obedient to God. Then spend some time in prayer, asking God to draw you into intimate communion with Himself and to transform your life so that you can affect the world for the sake of His kingdom.

Life Lessons to Remember

- ❧ Through brokenness, you gain a new perspective of God's mercy and provision (see Psalm 73:25–26).
- ❧ Through brokenness, you develop a more complete comprehension of yourself (see Psalm 73:21–23).
- ❧ Through brokenness, your compassion and understanding for the suffering of others grows (see Hebrews 5:2).

Whatever You Acquire Outside of God's Will Eventually Turns to Ashes

"Because you ... rejoiced in heart with all your disdain
for the land of Israel ... I will stretch out My hand
against you, and give you as plunder to the nations."

EZEKIEL 25:6–7

Life's Questions

The temptation sits before you, beckoning you to come take it. It looks so much like the desire of your heart that you can't stop thinking about it. An alarm goes off within your spirit. Something just isn't right about what you want to do. Still, the opportunity is so enticing that you are tempted to shake off the warning. You say to yourself, *Why shouldn't I have this? After all, other people have so much more. God doesn't really care about this, does He?*

Your spirit sends off another warning signal. God's Word makes it clear that He *does* care. You also know that you are up against a skilled opponent when it comes to deceit. He has a plan that he has tested and perfected over ages. But then you look again at that thing you want, and the argument continues. *What if this is my only chance to be happy? God wouldn't deny me that, would He? What if God never gives me what I really want?*

The truth is that the source of your temptation—the object that seems like the desire of your heart—will never satisfy you. Instead, it will lead you into dangerous territory outside of God's will for your life. This is why you must always remember Life Principle 16: *Whatever you acquire outside of God's will eventually turns to ashes.*

For hundreds of years, the Ammonites conspired to run the people of God out of the Promised Land (see Judges 3; 10–12; 2 Samuel 10; 1 Chronicles 19–20; 2 Chronicles 27:5; Psalm 3:3–8). So, when God rebuked the people of Judah for their sin, He simply took His hand of protection off of His people and allowed the Ammonites to attack. Still, God is just. He faithfully judged Ammon for its sinfulness (see Jeremiah 49:1–6; Ezekiel 21:28–32; 25:1–7; Amos 1:13–15).

What the Bible Says

1. Read Zephaniah 2:8. What was Ammon's intention regarding the people of God?

2. Read Ezekiel 21:28–32. The Ammonites found an ally in the Babylonians. How did God warn the Ammonites against helping the Babylonians?

3. How did the Babylonians convince the Ammonites to help them (see verse 29)?

4. Read 2 Kings 24:1–4. Why do you think the Ammonites failed to heed God's warning?

5. Read Ezekiel 25:1–7. What was particularly distressing about the Ammonites' attitudes as they plundered Judah (see verses 3, 6)? What was God's response (see verses 4–7)?

What It Means

The Ammonites were descendants of Lot, Abraham's nephew (see Genesis 12:5; 19:36–38), so they were both neighbors of Judah and Israel and related to them as well. The Ammonites could have learned to honor God and enjoy His blessings. Unfortunately, they were more interested in possessing the land of their relatives than in knowing their God. For this reason, they came to a bitter end: no land, no God, no nation—nothing. Everything they had turned to ashes, even though God gave them ample time to repent. Don't make the same mistake.

———— ⌇ ————

The Babylonian King Nebuchadnezzar betrayed Ammon, attacking its capital city around 581 BC. Ammon never recovered, and eventually the nation died out. During the third century BC, Ptolemy II Philadelphus renamed the city Philadelphia. It received its current name—Amman, Jordan—in the third century AD.

Life Examples

1. Read 1 Corinthians 3:8–15. When you became a Christian, what role did you take on (see verses 8–11; see also Ephesians 2:19–22)?

2. What must you constantly have in mind as you go about your day (see verse 11)?

3. What different motivations are there for doing work (see verses 12–13; see also 4:5)?

4. What type of work will endure (see verse 14)? What will be burned up?

5. Read 1 Peter 1:13–21. What is Peter's challenge to you?

Living the Principle

What do you long for? Love, wealth, acceptance, stability, prominence, or something else? If you chase after it apart from God's will, what you'll find once you achieve your goal will be disappointing and empty. It will burn up and turn to ashes—and it will singe you in the process as well. Therefore, don't ignore the alarm signal within you. It is God's Holy Spirit warning you that you're about to do something you will regret.

Instead, trust God and be holy as He is holy (see 1 Peter 1:15–16). Resist the temptation to go after the desire of your heart in your own strength. Remember that God will provide the absolute best for you if you trust and obey Him. Those blessings will endure, and they will be to God's glory in eternity. As David wrote, "You will show me the path of life; in Your presence is fullness of joy; at Your right hand are pleasures forevermore" (Psalm 16:11).

"Delight yourself also in the LORD, and He shall give you the desires of your heart" (Psalm 37:4).

How will you live out Life Principle 16 this week? Do you believe that God's will is truly the best for you? Why or why not? Think about the ways in which you are seeking God's will and the ways that you can resist temptation when it beckons to you. Then spend some time in prayer, asking God to draw you into intimate communion with Himself and to transform your life so that you can affect the world for the sake of His kingdom.

Life Lessons to Remember

- When you pursue your desires in opposition to God's will, you end up truly disappointed (see Psalm 106:15).
- As you pursue God, He fulfills the desires that He has given you (see Psalm 37:5).
- God's path offers pleasures and fulfillment that last forever (see Psalm 16:11).

LIFE PRINCIPLE 17

You Stand Tallest and Strongest On Your Knees

In his upper room, with his windows open toward Jerusalem, he knelt down on his knees three times that day, and prayed and gave thanks before his God.

DANIEL 6:10

Life's Questions

Following God isn't easy. The world that persecuted the prophets and crucified Christ still responds negatively to those who are committed to the Lord. Jesus explains the reason: "If they persecuted Me, they will also persecute you. . . . All these things they will do to you for My name's sake, because they do not know Him who sent Me. If I had not come and spoken to them, they would have no sin, but now they have no excuse for their sin" (John 15:20–22).

When others see God working through you, they will be convicted of their sin—and this will make them uncomfortable. This means they may lash out at you or try to undermine your testimony. They may do this in subtle ways, such as by making condescending remarks against you. They may decide not to let their children play with your kids. They may look for other ways to put you down, pull you into a verbal fight, or tarnish your reputation.

Have you encountered trouble because you're a Christian? Have you found it difficult to get along with particular people or in certain situations because you follow God? If so, you can discover the way that the saints before you defended themselves. In particular, as Life Principle 17 teaches, *You stand tallest and strongest on your knees.*

Daniel was of royal birth but was taken captive to Babylon as a young man. He was an impressive individual and was quickly recruited to serve in the king's palace (see Daniel 1:3-4), where he was careful to continue honoring and obeying God in every way. He ministered throughout the Babylonian captivity and shortly thereafter (c. 605 BC to 530 BC).

What the Bible Says

1. Read Daniel 6:1-9. How did Daniel distinguish himself? How did the king reward him for it (see verse 3)?

2. Why do you think the governors and satraps wanted to get rid of Daniel? What plot did they invent to trap him (see verses 4–8)?

3. Read Daniel 6:10–17. Why did Daniel disobey the decree (see verse 10)? In view of the plot against him, why wasn't he more secretive about praying to God?

4. How did the king react to hearing that Daniel had violated the decree (see verses 14, 16)?

5. Read Daniel 6:18–28. How did God honor Daniel's faithfulness (see verse 22)? What ultimately came from his obedience to God (see verses 26–28)?

What It Means

The strength of Daniel's character came from his time alone with God. He remained steadfast because he was consistent in praying to God and obeying His commands. His eyes were not on his foes or the ravenous lions. He did not worry about pandering to the governors and satraps, or try to gain points with the king. Rather, Daniel's attention was on God. He knew that he could not go wrong as long as he was honoring God, because his Lord would defend him.

Life Examples

1. What connection can you draw between Daniel's "excellent spirit" (verse 3), his faithfulness, and his daily prayer routine?

2. What does Daniel's story tell you about people who lead godly lives?

3. Read 1 Peter 5:6–11. What is God's promise to you if you obey Him (see verse 6)?

4. What "lion" do you have to watch out for when you submit yourself to God (see verse 8)?

5. From Daniel's example and verse 9, what have you learned about fighting the enemy? What will result from your obedience (see verses 10–11)?

What will your submission to God do? It will *perfect* you, which means to *restore, mend, render complete*, and *equip*. It will *establish* you, which means to *make as solid as granite, make stable, place firmly*, and *render constant*. It will *strengthen* you, which means to make strong or *fill with strength*. And it will *settle* you, which means to *lay the foundation of your faith and your future with Christ*.

Living the Principle

Being on your knees before God isn't just a physical stance. It's an attitude of the heart in which you are seeking God and are willing to submit to His plan for your future. As you spend time with Him in prayer, your relationship with God becomes deeper and more intimate. You feel His power and begin to trust Him in every situation. Instead of worrying about the "lions" in your path, you focus on Him and how He is working. This gives you the assurance and boldness to face your troubles, because you're confident that His plan for you will be accomplished.

Prayer is the most powerful thing that you can do. As difficult conflicts arise, the enemy may try to convince you to "tone down" your public devotion to the Lord or keep your walk with God a secret altogether. However, God will call you to a deeper walk with Him so that you can experience His provision, grow in your faith, and be a shining example to others.

"He is the living God, and steadfast forever; His kingdom is the one which shall not be destroyed, and His dominion shall endure to the end. He delivers and rescues, and He works signs and wonders in heaven and on earth" (Daniel 6:26–27).

How will you live out Life Principle 17 this week? The truth is that you stand tallest and strongest on your knees because that is when you *submit* yourself to God. Will you commit yourself to Him in prayer? Think about ways you can deepen your time alone with the Lord. Then spend some time in prayer, asking God to draw you into intimate communion with Himself and to transform your life so that you can affect the world for the sake of His kingdom.

Life Lessons to Remember

- God is greater than any problem you could ever face (see 1 John 4:4).
- Whatever you face, you must trust God with it (see 2 Samuel 22:2–4).
- God invites you to experience the awesome power of prayer (see Jeremiah 33:3).

LIFE PRINCIPLE 18

As a Child of a Sovereign God, You Are Never a Victim of Your Circumstances

"The children of Israel shall abide many days without king or prince . . . afterward the children of Israel shall return and seek the LORD their God."

HOSEA 3:4–5

Life's Questions

Large-scale tragedies, such as natural disasters, pandemics, or terrorist attacks, often inspire heated debate about God's presence. "Where is God in all this suffering?" people ask. "How could He allow something like this to happen? Doesn't He care about our world?" When global crises arise, such questions are as inevitable as they are challenging.

Yet their impact pales in comparison to the doubts and emotions that arise within *you* when a tragedy hits close to home. When an unexpected trial strikes you with a force that knocks you off your feet, the pain and loss may be far more intense than you ever thought possible. In your darkest moments, you may question your ability to survive. Stunned and overwhelmed, your mind will look for some explanation to which you can cling. You may wonder, *What did I do to deserve this? Why would God allow this to happen to me?*

During these times of heartbreak, you may not know why this adversity has come into your life. However, you can always trust that God is with you and loves you. You can place your faith in His unfailing character, His unfathomable wisdom, and the fact that He is always in control. For as Life Principle 18 states: *As a child of a sovereign God, you are never a victim of your circumstances.*

———————— ∞ ————————

Hosea was a prophet in the northern kingdom of Israel c. 755 BC to 715 BC. God brought His judgment to the kingdom of Judah through Babylon, and He judged Israel through the Assyrian invasion.

What the Bible Says

1. Read Hosea 1:1–3. What did the Lord command Hosea to do? What do you think the Lord's purpose was in giving this assignment to Hosea (see verse 2)?

2. Read Hosea 2:6–8, 13. What was God's judgment concerning Israel's unfaithfulness? What was Israel supposed to learn from God's rebuke (see verses 7–8)?

The Hebrew word for *master* or *owner* is *Ba'al*. The Lord is your true Master and Owner. However, you always need to be careful that your full affection is set on Him so that something else—such as wealth, relationships, power, or status—doesn't control you and become your god.

3. Read Hosea 2:14–20. What would God do *after* He judged Israel's sin (see verses 14–15)?

4. What does this passage tell you about God's intentions toward you (see verses 19–20)?

Hosea loved and cared for Gomer, yet she went
back to prostitution and was enslaved to another
man. Hosea was then forced to purchase her for half
the price of a female slave (see Exodus 21:32).

---

5. Read Hosea 3:1–5. How was God's relationship with Israel reflected in Hosea's relationship with Gomer? What did God say the people of Israel would ultimately do (see verse 5)?

What It Means

Through Hosea's marriage to Gomer, God gave the Israelites a picture of what He wanted to teach them. The people had sinned, abandoning the God who redeemed them from Egypt to run after false deities. Still, God loved His people and was committed to the covenant He had made with them. He was willing to take drastic measures—even allowing Assyria to invade them—to bring Israel back into a relationship with Himself. In fact, Hosea 3:5 says, "Afterward the children of Israel shall return and seek the LORD their God and David their king." This meant they would embrace the descendant of David who would become their Messiah. Through this conflict with Assyria, God would prepare the people of Israel for Jesus to be their Savior.

Life Examples

1. Read Psalm 103:19. What does God rule over? Is there anything in all creation that God does not control? Explain.

2. How does this apply to the trial that you are experiencing?

3. Read Hebrews 12:1–2. What is the key to running the "race" that God has set before you in spite of your circumstances?

4. How has looking to Christ enabled you to persevere in the midst of difficulties?

5. As far as you can tell right now, what kind of race has been set before you? How has endurance proved necessary in that race?

Living the Principle

God is sovereign, which means that everything that touches your life must serve some purpose. Nothing that happens to you is ever meaningless or useless. You are never merely a victim of an unfair world. God has an important purpose for refining you, which is to conform you to the image of His Son and glorify Himself through you. The more jolting the hardship, the greater the ministry for which God is preparing you. The deeper the cut, the more profoundly God will use you to do His work in the world if you will trust and obey Him.

Are you in the middle of a trial? Do you wonder why God has allowed such a painful experience in your life? If so, ask Him—in a humble and respectful manner—why He permitted the adversity and what He wants you to learn from it. Avoid becoming bitter and resentful. Always remember that God is ultimately in control, His love for you never changes, and His will for your life is good. You are not a victim. You are God's beloved child. He has an extraordinary plan for your life, so have faith in Him.

How will you live out Life Principle 18 this week? Consider how it helps you to know that God has a purpose in all of your circumstances. Then spend some time in prayer, asking God to draw you into intimate communion with Himself and to transform your life so that you can affect the world for the sake of His kingdom.

Life Lessons to Remember

- Your sovereign God has determined to use everything that happens to you for your blessing and His glory (see Romans 8:28).
- You can find comfort and encouragement in the lives of saints who trusted God in the face of adversity (see Hebrews 11).
- To endure, you must keep your eyes on Jesus (see Hebrews 12:1–3).

LIFE PRINCIPLE 19

Anything You Hold Too Tightly, You Will Lose

"They shall now go captive as the first of the captives, and those who recline at banquets shall be removed."

AMOS 6: 7

Life's Questions

What do you consider to be an absolute necessity in your life? What could you not live without? What would utterly devastate you if you lost it? Is it a relationship, possession, or a certain situation in your life? Is it more important to you than God? You need to consider how tight a hold it actually has on you, because it could become counterproductive and even dangerous. What would you do if God asked you to give it up? Could you obey Him? Does the thought of letting it go cause you to feel anxious and out of control?

For some people, money is central—they devote most of their time, energy, and attention to gaining it and keeping it. They regard wealth as the key to their worth, power, and prestige, and the thought of losing it keeps them up at night. Perhaps you feel you don't fall into this camp, but consider this question: *How much time do you spend each day thinking about your finances as compared to meditating on God's Word?*

If there is something that could keep you from trusting and honoring the Lord, it is an idol, and God is not going to allow you to keep it in your grasp. If you are looking to *anything* other than God for your sense of acceptance, accomplishment, and security, you are headed for serious trouble, because it will not last. Sooner or later, you will come to understand what Life Principle 19 teaches: *Anything you hold too tightly, you will lose.*

Amos was a shepherd and farmer in Judah who warned Israel about God's coming judgment (c. 760 BC to 750 bc). King Jeroboam II had expanded Israel's territory and wealth, but the prosperity corrupted the people and they became even more immoral and idolatrous.

What the Bible Says

1. Read Amos 2:6–8. How were the Israelites displeasing to the Lord?

2. Read Amos 6:1–8. In what were the Israelites placing their trust (see verse 1)?

3. What attitude were the people of Israel exhibiting (see verses 4–5)?

4. What do you think the *affliction of Joseph* was (see verse 6; see also Ezekiel 34:2–4)?

5. What did God hate about Israel's behavior (see verse 8; see also Psalm 10:2–4)? What was God's punishment (see verse 7)?

What It Means

The Israelites were so enamored with their prosperity that they forgot God (see Hosea 10:1–3). They had become prideful in their affluence and military victories and believed that they didn't need Him anymore. So when God called them to repentance, they refused to obey His commands or let Him back into their lives. They just weren't willing to give up their wealth and ease for Him—and in the end, it cost them everything.

Life Examples

1. Read 2 Kings 17:5–20. How did Amos' prophecy come true (see verses 5–6)?

2. How had God warned the people of their evil ways (see verse 13)?

3. How does God use similar methods today to warn people about their sinfulness?

4. How did the Israelites respond to God (see verses 14–17)?

5. What happened to everything the Israelites were trying to grasp
(see verses 18–20)?

Israel's capital, Samaria, was destroyed in 722 BC by
Assyria. Thousands of Israelites were taken captive to
Media and Upper Mesopotamia. The rest were made to
live under Assyrian rule, and Israel itself ceased to exist.
From there, the land changed hands many times, and
Israel did not become a nation again until May 14, 1948.

Living the Principle

God sent prophets to Israel and Judah before sending His judgment
(see Amos 3:7). As we discussed in Life Principle 10, *He will move heaven
and earth to show you His will.* God wants you to know what is going on
and what His plan is for you. However, no matter what the circumstances may be, your most important responsibility is to trust and
obey Him. If there is something you are honoring above God, He will
let you know that it displeases Him and He will call you to lay that
person, possession, or situation down on your own.

God will not share the control of your life with something or
someone else. Jesus said, "No one can serve two masters; for either he
will hate the one and love the other, or else he will be loyal to the one
and despise the other" (Matthew 6:24). You neither honor God nor
help yourself by having a divided heart. Therefore, make a decision

about what will rule your life once and for all. Surrender whatever is coming between you and the Lord. The good news is that no matter what God requires you to give up, you can be certain that your life is going to be much better without it in the long run. God is not punishing you by taking this precious thing from you—He is preparing to give you something even better.

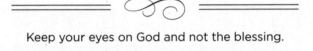

Keep your eyes on God and not the blessing.

How will you live out Life Principle 19 this week? Think about what you are having trouble giving up in your life and how you can instead choose to honor God. Then spend some time in prayer, asking God to draw you into intimate communion with Himself and to transform your life so that you can affect the world for the sake of His kingdom.

Life Lessons to Remember

- God loves you too much to allow any notions of self-sufficiency or dependence on anything other than Himself (see 2 Corinthians 12:7–10).
- Only God has the credentials to assume control of your life (see Psalm 139:13–16).
- Trusting God is the ideal antidote to fear and insecurity (see Psalm 56:3–4).

LIFE PRINCIPLE 20

Disappointments Are Inevitable; Discouragement Is a Choice

"Though the fig tree may not blossom, nor fruit be on the vines . . .
Yet I will rejoice in the LORD, I will joy in the God of my salvation."
HABAKKUK 3:17–18

Life's Questions

Life often doesn't turn out the way that you think it should. In fact, it rarely does. If you're like most people, your hopes and expectations almost always exceed your reality. Opportunities that you were counting on don't turn out the way that you thought they would. People that you thought you could depend on end up letting you down. Even the plans and expectations that you designed for yourself have been frustrated. It's all very disappointing.

What hopes do you have for your life? What opportunities, relationships, or situations are you constantly reaching for? What are you asking God to make a reality for you? There's nothing wrong with having such hopes and dreams. They serve as motivators that inspire you to strive for the best. But the harder you strive to fulfill your hopes and dreams, the greater your potential for disappointment if they don't come to pass.

During those times of disillusionment, will you allow your disappointments to dishearten you? Will you allow them to impede you from becoming everything God created you to be? Or will you rise up, learn from those setbacks in your life, and move on? The decision is yours, so choose wisely and remember the words of Life Principle 20: *Disappointments are inevitable; discouragement is a choice.*

The prophet Habakkuk ministered in Judah c. 612 BC to 588 BC, before and during the Babylonian invasion.

What the Bible Says

1. Read Zephaniah 1:2–6. What was happening in Judah before the Babylonians invaded?

2. Read Habakkuk 1:1–6. What was Habakkuk's reaction to the idolatry, immorality, and injustice he saw daily in his nation? What was God's response to him (see verses 5–6)?

3. Read Habakkuk 2:2–4. Why does God tell Habakkuk to write down His judgment concerning Babylon (see verses 2–3)?

4. What is God's admonition to Habakkuk (see verse 4)?

5. Read Habakkuk 3:17–19. How does Habakkuk respond to God?

The people of Judah were serving *fertility* gods—the basis for their idolatry was to increase their crops and prosperity. Habakkuk names all of the major crops of the region and says that, even if they all fail, God is still worthy of praise. That is the true heart of faith.

What It Means

Life can be depressing at times. Habakkuk pleaded for God to rebuke the wickedness of his countrymen, but was disheartened when he discovered the judgment would come in the form of a Babylonian invasion. This is the very core of disappointment—you expect something that will improve your circumstances, but you receive something that makes your situation worse. Yet even though Habakkuk didn't understand God's ways, he still trusted in God's wisdom. "I will rejoice in the Lord, I will joy in the God of my salvation. The Lord God is my strength" (Habakkuk 3:18–19). This is what you must do as well, even when God's answer to your prayers isn't what you were hoping for. Trust Him, because He knows exactly what He is doing.

Life Examples

1. Read Psalm 73:1–12. When have you doubted God because you saw someone else prospering in a manner that you've longed for?

2. Read Psalm 73:13–17. Have you ever been tempted to give up out of discouragement? If so, what was that time like for you?

3. What brought you back into fellowship with God after that time of discouragement?

4. Read Psalm 73:21–28. As a believer, what do you have to rely on when all else fails?

5. How can remembering this truth keep you from becoming discouraged?

Living the Principle

How do you respond when disappointments come your way? Do you become angry, frustrated, and disheartened? Or do you say, "Lord, I may not know why You allowed this, but I trust You, knowing that Your best for my life is still ahead." If you respond with discouragement and resentment, you will begin a downhill slide away from God's purpose for your life. However, if you respond with trust and praise, it will build your faith and bring you closer to the Lord.

Whenever you face disappointments, remember that your situation is in God's hand and under His sovereign control. Meditate on the fact that He loves you unconditionally and is providing His very best for you. Recall the blessings He has already given you. No matter what disappointments come, use them as stepping-stones to greater faith. Instead of becoming discouraged, you'll be filled with His courage, and there's nothing more encouraging than that.

"The Lord himself goes before you and will be with you;
he will never leave you nor forsake you. Do not be afraid;
do not be discouraged" (Deuteronomy 31:8 NIV).

How will you live out Life Principle 20 this week? Think about the disappointments you've experienced recently and how you can turn them to your advantage by trusting God. Then spend some time in prayer, asking God to draw you into intimate communion with Himself and to transform your life so that you can affect the world for the sake of His kingdom.

Life Lessons to Remember

- God has a unique plan for your life that is not changed by unexpected circumstances (see Isaiah 41:9–10).
- Whenever a situation arises that does not line up with your understanding of God's will, you must stop and look to Him for direction (see Psalm 32:8).
- God holds your future in His hands, and you will never lose by looking forward to what He has in store (see Philippians 3:13–14).

LIFE PRINCIPLE 21

Obedience Always Brings Blessing

He said, "More than that, blessed are those who
hear the word of God and keep it!"

LUKE 11:28

Life's Questions

How far does God expect you to go in your obedience to Him? Perhaps you've accepted Jesus as your Lord and Savior and have submitted some important areas to Him, but you're still not certain that you want to turn *every* part of your life over to Him. Maybe you fear that God will lead you in a direction you don't want to go or ask you to give up something you want to keep. Or perhaps procrastination has hindered your efforts to submit to God completely.

It could also be that you don't see the need to give God control over every part of your life. After all, didn't Paul say that "all things are lawful" for those in Christ (1 Corinthians 6:12)? If salvation comes through faith in Jesus and you can't lose it, why do you need to obey

God's truly difficult commands? However, don't miss the rest of Paul's message: "All things are lawful . . . but I will not be brought under the power of any. . . . For you were bought at a price; therefore glorify God in your body and in your spirit, which are God's" (verses 12, 20).

God wants you to enjoy the freedom that He gives you in every area (see Galatians 5:1, 13; James 1:25). But the only way to attain that liberty is through obedience. That's why Life Principle 21 teaches, *Obedience always brings blessing.*

When people questioned the power by which Jesus cast out demons, He replied, "If I cast out demons with the finger of God, surely the kingdom of God has come upon you" (Luke 11:20). Jesus provides the only way that a person can be free, but He requires our obedience in the process.

What the Bible Says

1. Read Luke 11:23–28. What does Jesus mean when He says, "He who is not with Me is against Me, and he who does not gather with Me scatters" (verse 23)?

2. Why can people turn to religions, rehabilitation programs, therapy, and the like and *appear* to get better, only to relapse into their old ways after a while (see verses 24–25)?

3. What do those belief systems and programs actually make room for (see verse 26)? What does this say about how Satan influences people's lives?

4. Can a person be *possessed* by a demon once Jesus Christ becomes their Savior and Lord (see 1 Corinthians 3:16; 6:17; 1 John 2:4)? Explain.

5. In what ways can you be *influenced* by the enemy (see 1 Corinthians 10:13; Ephesians 4:27; James 1:14)? What does Jesus admonish you to do (see Luke 11:28)?

As a "new creation" in Christ (2 Corinthians 5:17), only the Holy Spirit can dwell in you (see 1 Corinthians 6:19–20). The enemy's unclean spirits no longer have a place in you.

What It Means

Satan wants to control and destroy you (see 2 Thessalonians 1:8–9) and will do whatever he can to keep you from realizing your need for salvation in Christ. Once you receive Jesus as your Savior and His

Holy Spirit comes to live in you, you can no longer be possessed by his demons or forced to do his will (see Ephesians 4:30; 2 Timothy 2:26). The only thing Satan can do is destroy your effectiveness for the kingdom of God and stop you from enjoying the relationship that you have with the Lord. The enemy does this by tempting you to sin. Whenever you *disobey* God, you participate in the enemy's plot to injure you and make you miserable. You also act *against* Christ rather than *with* Him. Jesus calls you to obedience so you may enjoy the abundant life He created you for (see John 10:10). This is why He gives you His Spirit, so "[you] might know the things that have been freely given to [you] by God" (1 Corinthians 2:12).

Life Examples

1. Read John 15:4–8. How do you produce something that is worthy and eternal (see verses 4–5)? What is Christ's promise to you if you obey Him faithfully (see verse 7; see also Psalm 37:4)?

The word *abide* in the New Testament means to remain steadfast, persevering in being united as one with Christ in heart, soul, mind, strength, and will. How do you remain so close to God? He will show you as you do what He says.

---

2. You exist to glorify God (see Psalm 86:8–12; Matthew 5:16); therefore, how do you best live out the purpose for which you were created (see verse 8)?

3. What kind of *fruit* is Jesus talking about (see Galatians 5:22–23; 1 Peter 1:5–8)? Do you exhibit these characteristics? Why or why not?

4. Read John 15:9–16. Why does Jesus have you join Him in doing His work in the world (see verse 11)? What should your motivation be in everything you do for God (see verses 9–10, 13–14)?

5. Why is it important to remember that you serve *with* God out of *friendship*, rather than *for* God out of *obligation* (see verses 15–16)?

Living the Principle

An additional aspect of this principle is that your obedience to God often blesses those closest to you. For instance, when a father obeys the Lord, his entire family may reap the reward of God's blessings. Likewise, a child's obedience to Christ may be a great gift to his or her parents. When you live an obedient life, those who know and love you can sense the peace and joy God has given you. Instead of conflict, there can be contentment.

God knows what is best for you, and He wants to see it accomplished in your life. So, what is hindering you from obeying Him? Are you holding on to a person, goal, or activity that is less than God's best? It may be frightening to submit it to the Lord, but do it anyway. He wants to bless you and give you freedom in that area, but He will only do so when you obey Him. While obedience is sometimes challenging, it will be worth it when you see God working in your life and experience. Therefore, obey God with confidence, knowing that you will be blessed when you do.

How will you live out Life Principle 21 this week? Consider any areas in which you are having trouble with obedience and be accountable to another person in turning those areas over to God. Then spend some time in prayer, asking God to draw you into intimate communion with Himself and to transform your life so that you can affect the world for the sake of His kingdom.

Life Lessons to Remember

- ↝ Obeying God in small matters is an essential step to receiving God's greatest blessings (see Mark 4:30–32).
- ↝ When you obey God, you will never be disappointed (see Psalm 22:5).
- ↝ Your obedience always benefits others (see 2 Corinthians 4:11–15).

LIFE PRINCIPLE 22

To Walk in the Spirit Is to Obey the Initial Promptings of the Spirit

While Peter thought about the vision, the Spirit said
to him, "Behold, three men are seeking you."
ACTS 10:19

Life's Questions

When you accepted Jesus as your Savior, several things happened. You received God's complete forgiveness, eternal life, and your old sin nature was replaced with a new nature that the Lord works through to conform you to the likeness of Christ. You also received the Holy Spirit, who is sent by Jesus to dwell within all those who believe in Him. It is His Holy Spirit who enables you to lead a godly life and is your sufficiency as you walk in the footsteps of Jesus.

With such provision, it may seem like the Christian life should be easy and joyful. But do you ever feel burned out in your walk with

God? Do you wonder if you are on the right track or if there is something more that you should be experiencing? Do you wish that God's direction were clearer to you? If so, it may be an indication that you are trying to live the Christian life in your own strength and wisdom rather than by following the leadership of God's Holy Spirit. Jesus called the Holy Spirit the "Spirit of truth" (John 14:17). He leads you to decisions, choices, and an understanding of God's will that is true from God's perspective.

The Holy Spirit empowers you to both know and keep God's commandments. He leads you and guides you—often in ways you don't expect—down ways that prove to be the most effective path. Your part is to act on His promptings. This is why Life Principle 22 teaches, *To walk in the Spirit is to obey the initial promptings of the Spirit.*

What the Bible Says

1. Read Acts 10:1–8. What sort of man was Cornelius (see verses 1–4)?

Cornelius was known as a *God-fearer.* This meant
that he ascribed to Jewish worship and morals
and believed in the One True God, but he probably
wasn't a Jewish convert in the formal sense of being
circumcised and undergoing Jewish baptism.

2. How specific was the Lord in His instruction to Cornelius (see verses 5–6)? Why do you think he was so moved by the vision (see verses 7–8)?

3. Read Acts 10:9–16. How was Peter's response different than Cornelius' (see verse 14)? Why do you think Peter answered as he did (see verse 14; also see Leviticus 11:4, 8)?

4. Read Acts 10:17–23. How quickly did the Spirit reveal to Peter what the vision meant?

5. Read Acts 10:24–48. How did Peter show that he had learned what God was teaching him through the vision (see verses 28, 34–35)?

"I am not ashamed of the gospel, because it is the power of God that brings salvation to everyone who believes: first to the Jew, then to the Gentile" (Romans 1:16 NIV).

6. How were the people blessed by the obedience of Peter and
Cornelius (see verses 44–45; also see 11:15–18)?

What It Means

Cornelius was among the first Gentiles to become part of the church
without first becoming a Jewish convert. Before this, it was thought
that Gentile believers could not receive the Holy Spirit because it was
only for the people of Israel. In other words, non-Jews were not considered full, complete Christians. Thankfully, neither Peter nor Cornelius
ignored the promptings of the Holy Spirit because of their precon-
ceived notions. Instead, their obedience opened the way for Gentiles
to become part of the body of Christ. Unless you have a Jewish back-
ground, you are directly affected by this event. You do not have to go
through all of the rituals of becoming a Jew before you can accept
Christ as your Savior and receive the Holy Spirit. And it's all because
two men were obedient to the promptings of the Spirit.

Life Examples

1. Read Acts 16:1–10. As the scene opens, Paul and Silas have
recently embarked on a missionary journey to visit the churches
that Paul previously planted. What was the immediate effect on
the churches they visited (see verse 5)?

2. How did the Holy Spirit direct Paul and Silas (see verses 6–7)?

3. Why did the Holy Spirit *prevent* them from preaching the gospel?

4. When has the Holy Spirit shut a door to you that you did not understand?

5. How did the Holy Spirit redirect Paul and Silas (see verses 9–10)?

———— ⟳ ————

This was Paul's second missionary journey. He may
have been looking forward to visiting the churches
that he'd previously planted, but God had other plans—
including crossing the Aegean Sea to a new continent
(Europe) to share the gospel. Once there, Paul planted
churches at Philippi, Thessalonica, and Berea.

Living the Principle

Have you been ignoring the Holy Spirit's promptings because you're unsure about where He is directing you? Has the Spirit challenged your beliefs? Is He moving you to change your course? The Holy Spirit can never lead you wrong, because He guides you in doing God's will—which is glorifying God and becoming everything that He created you to be.

Jesus said, "The Spirit . . . will guide you into all truth . . . He will glorify Me, for He will take of what is Mine and declare it to you" (John 16:13–14). The Holy Spirit is your Counselor, Comforter, and Helper, and He makes sure that you have everything you need to accomplish whatever God has called you to do. Therefore, you need to stop trying to do everything by your own power. Obey what the Holy Spirit is guiding you to do right away, and then watch and enjoy the wonderful Spirit-filled life that unfolds before you.

How will you live out Life Principle 22 this week? Think about the challenges and blessings that come with obeying the initial promptings of the Holy Spirit. Then spend some time in prayer, asking God to draw you into intimate communion with Himself and to transform your life so that you can affect the world for the sake of His kingdom.

Life Lessons to Remember

- ❧ You must stay yielded to the Holy Spirit (see Romans 8:13–14).
- ❧ You must trust the Holy Spirit to guide you (see 1 Thessalonians 5:19).
- ❧ You must listen for the Holy Spirit's promptings (see Galatians 5:16–18).

LIFE PRINCIPLE 23

You Can Never Outgive God

God is able to make all grace abound toward you,
that you, always having all sufficiency in all things,
may have an abundance for every good work.

2 CORINTHIANS 9:8

Life's Questions

Giving is an aspect of discipleship that pastors are generally hesitant to talk about and believers are usually less than enthusiastic to learn. For some reason, the topics of tithing and generosity strike us as too personal to discuss and are often difficult to turn over to the Lord. We're eager to receive God's blessings, yet we're hesitant to obey Him with the gifts that He's given us. This is often due to a lack of trust and the refusal to acknowledge God's ownership of all that exists.

Yet the Bible is filled from cover to cover with stories about God's goodness. He is always giving, always loving, and always being generous toward His children. In Genesis, He gives Adam and Eve a perfect

Garden of Eden. In Revelation, He reveals the ultimate home He has prepared for His children—a perfect and eternal heaven. In the books in between, we find that He delights in blessing His people and that He sent His Son as His ultimate gift to us.

God is loving and full of grace, so when He commands you to let go of your wealth and resources, it is for a good reason. He does not want to deprive you but to teach you to be more like Him by making you into a generous giver. As you learn to let go of your possessions, you uncover the truth of Life Principle 23: *You can never outgive God.*

What the Bible Says

1. Read Acts 11:27–30. Why did the disciples find it necessary to send aid to the believers in Judea—and, more specifically, the church in Jerusalem (see verse 28)?

2. Read 2 Corinthians 8:1–7. What example had the Macedonian churches set (see verses 1–4)? Why do you think Paul begins his plea to the Corinthians by first citing this positive example of the Macedonians (see verse 7)?

God sent Paul to the Macedonians during his second
missionary journey, and this letter to the Corinthians
was written during his third missionary journey, a few
years later. Paul couldn't have known what an immense
blessing the Macedonian churches would be to him
and to the church in Jerusalem—but God did.

---

3. Read 2 Corinthians 8:8–15. Why is it often easier to show your love and support for others in ways that are not financial (see verse 8)?

4. When have you pledged to donate resources but then failed to make good on your promise (see verses 10–12)? What happened as a result?

The Corinthians had pledged to give to the church in
Jerusalem but had not yet fulfilled their promise.

---

5. Why is it in your interest to be faithful to God with your finances and to show generosity toward others (see verses 13–15; also see Malachi 3:10; Luke 6:38; Galatians 5:13–15)?

What It Means

Along with the famine (see Acts 11:27–30), there were other factors affecting the poor in Jerusalem. Many believers had been disowned by their families and community and lost the ability to support themselves. This led to the pooling of resources, which were soon spent (see Acts 2:44; 4:34). There were also many widows that needed to be supported (see Acts 6:1–6), as well as missionaries that were being sent out. To make matters even worse, the people were being taxed by Jewish and Roman authorities, which meant it was nearly impossible to produce enough to live on. However, through these financial troubles, God was teaching the Gentile believers to show His love to others, and He was also showing Jewish believers that they could trust the Gentile Christians. God was uniting a church that was divided by culture and distance.

Life Examples

1. Read 2 Corinthians 9:1–15. What do you think Paul told the Macedonians about the Corinthians (see verse 2)?

2. When people think of you as a good example, does it motivate you to act in a godly manner, even if it's difficult (see verses 3–5)? Why or why not?

3. How have you seen the principle in verse 6 proven true in your own life?

4. On what is cheerful giving based (see verse 7; also see Matthew 10:8; John 13:34; 1 Corinthians 13:3; Ephesians 5:2)?

5. What is God's promise to you when you give (see verse 8)? What does obedience to God in your finances inspire (see verses 10–15)?

⸺ ❧ ⸺

The word *grace* in the New Testament comes from the root word *to rejoice*. It means *the absolutely free benefit or expression of loving-kindness, deeds which cause joy, and favor conferred*. When Paul writes, "God is able to make all grace abound toward you" (2 Corinthians 9:8), it means that God shows you a superabundance of kindness that will cause you immense joy.

Living the Principle

Do you give ten percent of your income for the ministry of the church? Do you give generously to bless those in need? Perhaps you think, *I can't because I have barely enough to live on myself.* Or maybe your response is, *I've worked hard for what I have and I don't see why I should give it up.* As we've discussed, both of these attitudes come from a lack of trust in God and the refusal to acknowledge His ownership of all that exists.

God wants to "open . . . the windows of heaven and pour out for you such blessing that there will not be room enough to receive it" (Malachi 3:10), but He will wait until you submit this area of your life to Him. He knows your struggles, desires, and the circumstances that surround your life, and He has promised to "supply all your need according to His riches in glory by Christ Jesus" (Philippians 4:19). So stop making decisions based on a balance sheet and start obeying God in every area—including your finances. You'll never come up short. Be generous with Him, and what you'll find are greater blessings than you could have imagined.

How will you live out Life Principle 23 this week? Consider the blessings of turning your finances over to God and commit to being accountable with another person in this area. Then spend some time in prayer, asking God to draw you into intimate communion with Himself and to transform your life so that you can affect the world for the sake of His kingdom.

Life Lessons to Remember

- All you have is a gift from God; therefore, whatever you offer Him is only a portion of what He has already given to you (see Deuteronomy 10:14).
- When you obey Him by honoring Him with your tithes, He protects your finances and blesses you (see Malachi 3:10).
- God supplies all your needs from His limitless wealth (see Philippians 4:19).

LIFE PRINCIPLE 24

To Live the Christian Life Is to Allow Jesus to Live His Life in and through You

*I have been crucified with Christ; it is no longer
I who live, but Christ lives in me.*
GALATIANS 2:20

Life's Questions

What troubles you today? What concern is consuming you with fear and doubt? Do you realize it's not your place to worry about that situation? Have you come to the understanding that everything that concerns you is Christ's responsibility to care for rather than yours, and that your job is simply to obey Him? As David wrote, "Though I walk in the midst of trouble . . . Your right hand will save me. The LORD will perfect that which concerns me" (Psalm 138:7–8).

Many people daydream of receiving an unexpected inheritance from a wealthy person. However, as a believer in Christ Jesus, you are the heir of the most lavish inheritance that any person could ever dream to receive! Paul declared, "Eye has not seen, nor ear heard, nor have entered into the heart of man the things which God has prepared for those who love Him" (1 Corinthians 2:9). The inheritance you have been given in Christ is so glorious, so vast, and so tremendous you cannot even comprehend it with your finite mind.

You may be so used to taking care of yourself and/or others that this is a difficult concept to accept. But if you don't grasp this truth, you will continue being distracted by issues that were never yours to worry about, and you will miss out on the blessings of the abundant life that God has planned for you. So instead, choose today to embrace Life Principle 24: *To live the Christian life is to allow Jesus to live His life in and through you.*

***

The Jerusalem Council (see Acts 15) was the first conference held by the early church. It addressed the concerns of the Judaizers, who trusted Jesus as their Savior but also believed that Christians should keep the law in order to attain salvation. Of course, Christ made no such requirement for salvation.

What the Bible Says

1. Read Acts 15:1–5 and Galatians 2:11–13. Why did Paul criticize Peter? What was the nature of the dispute?

2. Read Galatians 2:14–21. What is Paul's counsel to Peter (see verse 14)? How is a person justified or saved (see verse 16; also see Acts 15:7–11)?

When Peter spoke of the salvation of the Gentiles, he
was referring to what had occurred as he was preaching
to Cornelius and his household (see Acts 10).

---

3. Why do you think our tendency is to be distracted by the law, good deeds, and religious activities (see verses 17–19)? What is the true proof you are saved (see verse 20)?

4. What does it mean to allow Christ to live through you? Is there anything specific that you should be doing (see verse 20; also see Romans 6:5–13)?

5. When you go back to living by the law or religious rituals instead of by God's grace, what are you really saying (see verse 21)?

What It Means

The Judaizers likely believed they were guarding the faith. However, what they were really doing was being distracted by issues that weren't important and creating conflict within the church. Peter rebuked them by saying, "Why do you test God by putting a yoke on the neck of the disciples which neither our fathers nor we were able to bear? But we believe that through the grace of the Lord Jesus Christ we shall be saved" (Acts 15:10–11). If there is something in your life distracting *you* from following God or creating a yoke of bondage that shouldn't be there, return to the basic truth that your salvation is through faith in Christ.

Life Examples

1. Read Matthew 16:24–27. What does it mean to take up your cross (see verse 24)?

2. How do you lose your life for Christ's sake (see verse 25)?

3. What life do you find when you do this (see verses 25–26)?

4. Why is it important that you guard your soul?

5. What promise do you have if you allow Christ to live through you (see verse 27)?

Living the Principle

God does not call you to an *adequate* life. He wants your life to be *extraordinary*. However, for you to experience the life He has planned for you, you must stop being distracted by peripheral issues and focus your attention completely on Him. Can you trust Jesus to live His life through you and take care of all that troubles you?

Of course you can! The God who saved you can teach you how to live for Him. The Lord who forgave your sins and gives you a home in heaven can surely attend to that person or situation that is causing you so much concern. And the Savior that you trusted for your eternity is more than capable of taking care of all the matters that burden you daily. Therefore, die to your worries so you can experience true life in Him.

═══════════ ⟨∾⟩ ═══════════

"Let us run with endurance the race that is set
before us, looking unto Jesus, the author and
finisher of our faith" (Hebrews 12:1–2).

═══════════════════════════════

How will you live out Life Principle 24 this week? Think about all the distractions that have been troubling you and submit them to God. Then spend some time in prayer, asking God to draw you into intimate communion with Himself and to transform your life so that you can affect the world for the sake of His kingdom.

Life Lessons to Remember

- There is nothing you can do to earn the gift of God's salvation and your new identity in Christ—it is given to you freely (see Ephesians 2:8–10).
- God desires an intimate, daily relationship with you in which you experience His presence, trust His wisdom, and rely on His strength (see Isaiah 58:2).
- The Spirit-filled life is marked by purpose, power, and effectiveness (see Romans 8:14–17).

LIFE PRINCIPLE 25

God Blesses You So That You Might Bless Others

Let him who stole steal no longer, but rather let him
labor, working with his hands what is good, that he
may have something to give him who has need.

EPHESIANS 4:28

Life's Questions

Does your love for God motivate you to serve others? Does your relationship with Him inspire you to comfort other people just as He has done for you? Every person needs encouragement at times, but for the most part this world is experiencing a drought of comforting words, uplifting examples, inspirational stories of God's goodness, and genuine expressions of appreciation. You are far more likely to hear negative words of criticism, blame, and ridicule on a daily basis than you are to hear positive words of praise, recognition, and thankfulness.

You may not feel that you have much to offer to people that will help them, but you do. In fact, there are many ways you can minister to others with the abilities and resources that God has given to you. If you know Jesus Christ as your Lord and Savior, you can share your faith with those who have never experienced forgiveness for their sin and don't know where they will spend eternity. If God has given you talents or provided you with a good income, you can help others with what you've been given. If God has taken you through a difficult situation and carried you to the other side, you can share your story with someone facing those same circumstances.

First Peter 4:10 teaches, "As each one has received a gift, minister it to one another, as good stewards of the manifold grace of God." Are you willing to be a good steward of what God has provided to you? Then look for opportunities to help others as you embrace Life Principle 25: *God blesses you so that you might bless others.*

What the Bible Says

1. Read Ephesians 4:1–6. What are the qualities of a life worthy of Christ (see verses 1–3; also see Colossians 3:12–13)? Why are these qualities important (see verses 4–6)?

Jesus poured out His life so that others could be saved (see Luke 19:10). If you're going to represent Him (see 2 Corinthians 5:20), shouldn't you be like Him in your character and purpose?

---

2. Read Ephesians 4:7–16. What did Christ give believers so they could bless one another (see verses 7–8)?

3. What is your spiritual gift (see verses 11–12; also see Romans 12:4–8)? Why has that gift been given to you (see verses 13–16)?

4. Read Ephesians 4:17–32. How should you view yourself and others? What should be your goal concerning others (see verses 21–24, 28–29; also see Philippians 2:1–4)?

5. Why do negative attitudes or selfish actions grieve the Holy Spirit (see verses 30–31; also see Romans 8:26–29)? What brings joy to the Holy Spirit (see verse 32)?

What It Means

Ephesus was a wealthy and influential city in Asia Minor. As Paul sat in prison (see Ephesians 3:1; 4:1; 6:20), he must have thought about the amazing influence for Christ the Ephesian believers could have on the world. However, he knew they first had to learn that their true wealth wasn't in earthly riches but in spiritual blessings by which they encouraged others (see Ephesians 1). Paul taught them to remember the words of Jesus, who said, "It is more blessed to give than to receive" (Acts 20:35). They needed to realize the reason God had given them such blessings was to use them for His glory and for the furtherance of the gospel. The same is true for you. God's gifts to you were never meant to be hoarded. They were given to be used wisely as you minister to others through the power and wisdom of the Holy Spirit.

"It is your Father's good pleasure to give you the kingdom. Sell what you have and give alms; provide yourselves money bags which do not grow old, a treasure in the heavens that does not fail, where no thief approaches nor moth destroys. For where your treasure is, there your heart will be also" (Luke 12:32–34).

Life Examples

1. Read 1 Corinthians 12:4–11. What makes you *different* from other believers (see verses 4–6)? How are you to be *like* other believers?

2. For whom does the Holy Spirit give you gifts, talents, and blessings (see verse 7)?

3. Why do you think the Holy Spirit wanted you personally to have the gifts that you've received (see verse 11)?

4. Read 1 Corinthians 12:12–19. Why are your gifts essential to the church?

5. How are you using your gifts in a way that honors God and blesses others?

Living the Principle

Who are the special people that God has used to shape your life? Do you ever consider how much they gave for you and how willingly they shared the gifts that God provided to them? They were faithful to bless you with what God had given them, and you should be, too.

Can you be trusted with the blessings that God has given you? Does your love for God motivate you to minister to others in His name and for His glory? Does your relationship with Him inspire you to give freely so that others can know His salvation, comfort, and joy? Only you can stop God's goodness from flowing through your life and into the lives of others—and you do it by hoarding His gifts. Therefore, count your blessings and look for opportunities to shine His light and love into other people's lives. Then step back and watch how God works. Soon you will see that it truly is much more blessed to give than to receive.

"If I am being poured out as a drink offering on the sacrifice and service of your faith, I am glad and rejoice with you all" (Philippians 2:17).

How will you live out Life Principle 25 this week? Think about ways that you can share your gifts and blessings with others. Then spend some time in prayer, asking God to draw you into intimate communion with Himself and to transform your life so that you can affect the world for the sake of His kingdom.

Life Lessons to Remember

- God saved you because He loves you (see Ephesians 1:3–6).
- God's purpose for saving you was to bring Him glory (see Matthew 5:16).
- You are most like Jesus when you serve others (see Matthew 20:27–28).

LIFE PRINCIPLE 26

Adversity Is a Bridge to a Deeper Relationship with God

I also count all things loss for the excellence of the knowledge of Christ . . . that I may know Him and the power of His resurrection, and the fellowship of His sufferings.

PHILIPPIANS 3:8, 10

Life's Questions

There's nothing more lonely than suffering, because it feels like no one understands what you're going through. When you have accomplishments and prosperity, loved ones will gather around to share in your joy and celebrate your success. But with grief, people feel distant—even when they are trying to support and comfort you— because they cannot reach into that profound place where your pain has made its home.

During those times, you may wonder, *Where is God? Why has God allowed this? Has He left me alone to struggle with this by myself? Has God abandoned me?* Yet just the opposite is true. Psalm 34:18 assures, "The LORD is near to those who have a broken heart, and saves such as have a contrite spirit." Adversity isn't a time when God is far from you. On the contrary, it is a time when He is the closest to you and is teaching you His ways.

When everything goes well, you may forget that you need God, but when trouble strikes, it's only God who can comfort you to the depth of your soul. He has your full attention and can teach you the joy of His wonderful presence. This is why Life Principle 26 teaches, *Adversity is a bridge to a deeper relationship with God.*

What the Bible Says

1. Read 2 Corinthians 11:23–31. What did Paul see as validating his ministry (see verse 23)? Why can Paul boast in his adversities and infirmities (see verse 30)?

2. Read Philippians 3:3–11. What does Paul say about putting confidence in earthly accomplishments—or "the flesh" (see verse 3)?

When Paul writes about the *flesh*, he is speaking of our human nature—our earthly desires and inclinations. Our flesh doesn't follow God. In fact, it's often completely opposed to the Holy Spirit (see Romans 7). Our flesh seeks carnal pleasures and finds importance in accomplishments, wealth, beauty, and so on. The Spirit, on the other hand, will always direct you to become more like Christ, placing His emphasis on obedience.

3. Why was Paul content with losing his earthly riches and honors (see verses 7–8)? What did Paul find in Christ that he couldn't obtain through possessions and titles (see verse 9)?

4. Why do you think Paul found true life when he was conformed to Christ's death (see verses 10–11; see also Mark 10:29–30)?

How precious and freeing it is to admit: *I need God!*

5. Read Philippians 3:12–21. What was Paul's goal (see verses 12–14; see also 1:13–14, 21–26)? What happens to those who do not share his focus but put their trust in earthly accomplishments and wealth (see verses 17–19)?

What It Means

Paul had everything that defined a successful and blessed life. From birth, he observed the law to the letter and grew to be a prominent Pharisee. He enjoyed social prominence. He could trace his lineage to Benjamin, the youngest son of Jacob, and was a descendant of Saul, the first king of Israel. He was born in Tarsus, which gave him all the rights and privileges of a Roman citizen. Few could match Paul's credentials and accomplishments. Yet no matter how pious or perfect he was, it was never enough. Paul needed Jesus. It wasn't through his success that he experienced God but through his suffering and adversity. And during those times, God touched him so profoundly and intimately that Paul realized how priceless it was to experience adversity (see Romans 5:3–5; 8:17–18; 2 Corinthians 1:3–11; 12:7–10; Colossians 1:24).

"I consider that the sufferings of this present time
are not worthy to be compared with the glory
which shall be revealed in us" (Romans 8:18).

Life Examples

1. Read 2 Corinthians 4:5–16. Why has God shone His light in our hearts (see verses 5–6)?

2. What then is the treasure we have in us as believers (see verse 7)?

3. Why does God allow imperfect people to carry His precious gospel (see verses 8–10)?

4. Who benefits most from our adversity (see verses 15–16)?

5. How has God used adversity to strengthen your faith and trust in Him?

Living the Principle

Your trials may be prolonged, intense, confusing, complicated, and stressful. At times, you may get frustrated, impatient, and even angry with God. However, the more fiercely you insist on holding on to your earthly sources of pleasure and accomplishment, the longer it will take for God to teach you that only He can heal your soul. And the farther you push Him away and rebel against Him, the more lengthy your time of affliction will be.

The wisest response to your troubles is to surrender your will to God and grow in your relationship with Him. Keep your focus on Him. Trust His love, wisdom, and strength. If you respond the right way, you will know Him more deeply and intimately, and His purpose will be accomplished in you. You will see His glory in a way that you never thought possible.

How will you live out Life Principle 26 this week? Have you experienced God's profound comfort and presence in your life? Think about the trials you are facing and how He is reaching deep within your soul to bring you closer to Himself. Then spend some time in prayer, asking God to draw you into intimate communion with Himself and to transform your life so that you can affect the world for the sake of His kingdom.

Life Lessons to Remember

- ❧ God's objective in adversity is to draw you closer to Himself (see 2 Corinthians 1:3–7).
- ❧ When adversity strikes, immediately turn to God (see Psalm 40:1–3).
- ❧ Adversity is a tool God uses to shape His servant for service (see 1 Peter 1:6–7).

LIFE PRINCIPLE 27

Prayer Is Life's Greatest Time-Saver

Finally, brethren, pray for us, that the word of the Lord
may run swiftly and be glorified, just as it is with you.
2 THESSALONIANS 3:1

Life's Questions

You wake up knowing you can't waste a second because there are so many demands on your life. Your heart and mind begin to race. *There just isn't enough time to get it all done,* you tell yourself. As your feet hit the floor, you are tempted to take off running so you can engage the frenzy of activity that awaits you. But that's exactly the *wrong* thing to do.

Before you throw yourself into the melee of busyness and nonstop competition for your attention, you need to take a moment to focus on your heavenly Father and engage with Him in prayer. Chances are that prayer is one of the things you've decided to sacrifice to squeeze a few more minutes into your day. You may think, *I'm sorry, God, I just can't stop.* But consider this a wake-up call. You cannot afford to leave God out of your planning.

If you want to make the most of every moment, you must begin your day with the One who holds every second of your life in His hands. As you do this on a consistent basis, you will come to discover the truth of Life Principle 27: *Prayer is life's greatest time-saver.*

What the Bible Says

1. Read 2 Thessalonians 1:3–12. What event is on Paul's mind as he writes to the Thessalonians (see verses 7–10)? What is his prayer for the believers (see verses 11–12)?

2. Read 2 Thessalonians 2:1–7. How would the Thessalonians know that the Day of Christ had arrived (see verses 3–4)?

The church at Thessalonica was a young, thriving
church that was composed mainly of Gentiles. However,
increasing persecution and false teachers who were
distorting the truth caused the Thessalonians to worry
that they had missed the Second Coming of Christ.

3. Read 2 Thessalonians 2:8–12. Why do you think God allows the lawless one to be revealed before the Lord destroys him (see verse 12; see also Matthew 13:41–43; 24:7–14)?

4. Read 2 Thessalonians 3:1–5. Knowing that Paul is thinking about the condemnation that awaits the unrighteous (see 2:12), what does he ask from the brethren (see verses 1–2)?

5. Instead of fretting about spreading the gospel, what does Paul draw confidence from (see verse 3)? What was he counting on concerning other believers (see verse 5)?

What It Means

Paul knew that Christ's command was for believers to be His witnesses "to the end of the earth" (Acts 1:8). He knew that before Christ returns, the "gospel of the kingdom will be preached in all the world" (Matthew 24:14). Jesus had told His disciples, "There are some standing here who shall not taste death till they see the kingdom of God" (Luke 9:27), and the increasing persecution of believers led many to believe Christ's return was imminent. There was so much to do—so many people to reach—that Paul must have felt overwhelmed by the task, especially with all the obstacles that confronted him. Yet he knew God could get it done. If he stayed in constant communication with the Lord through prayer, God would maximize his time and give him the wisdom and energy needed to accomplish his part of the mission.

Life Examples

1. Read Philippians 4:4–7. Why does Paul encourage you to remain calm, gentle, and joyful in the Lord (see verses 4–6)?

2. What are you to do instead of fretting over your troubles (see verse 6)?

3. Why does giving your concerns over to God give you peace (see verse 7)?

4. Read Proverbs 2:1–9. What are the characteristics of a person who wants to receive wisdom and understanding from God (1–5)?

5. How does a pattern of listening to God enable you to understand "righteousness and justice, equity and every good path" (verse 9)?

"Certainly God has heard me; He has attended to the voice of my prayer. Blessed be God, who has not turned away my prayer, nor His mercy from me!" (Psalm 66:19–20).

Living the Principle

Whatever it is you need to accomplish may seem overwhelming and unfeasible to you. However, "things which are impossible with men are possible with God" (Luke 18:27). God knows everything that will happen to you today, and He knows the best way for you to handle your tasks. Therefore, you must spend time listening to Him in prayer, receiving His wisdom and direction, and drinking in His presence and power.

Be quiet before Him, rest in Him, and allow Him to order your steps. He will keep you from moving in the wrong direction or from wasting your time doing meaningless and useless things. He will slow you down to accomplish the activities that require caution and precision and give you the speed to move through the things that are less important. He will also steer you clear of the time traps you should avoid. Whether you face a calm day or one full of activity, commit yourself to His schedule and guidance through prayer. You'll find that your time with God is the best investment that you make every day.

God will answer our prayers as soon as it is best for us.

How will you live out Life Principle 27 this week? Think about times when you've committed your day to God and He accomplished amazing things through you. Then spend some time in prayer, asking God to draw you into intimate communion with Himself and to transform your life so that you can affect the world for the sake of His kingdom.

Life Lessons to Remember

- Go to God first before making decisions (see Matthew 6:33).
- Commit to seeking God's instructions each day (see Daniel 6:10).
- Listen for God's direction when you pray (see Jeremiah 33:3).

LIFE PRINCIPLE 28

No Christian Has Ever Been Called to "Go It Alone" in His or Her Walk of Faith

And let us consider one another in order to stir up
love and good works, not forsaking the assembling of
ourselves together, as is the manner of some.
HEBREWS 10:24–25

Life's Questions

There are many reasons why people do not attend church. Some refuse to join because they've had a terrible experience with "religious" people. Others live far away from a congregation and don't feel it is feasible to be active members. At times, people are shy and find it difficult to open up to others, or they have so many responsibilities they don't think they have the energy to participate adequately. There are also those who are so frightened of being rejected that they isolate themselves from others—including other Christians.

And recently, a new temptation has arisen. Many people have become accustomed to online church—staying at home and watching sermons through popular streaming platforms or via podcasts. We can listen to our favorite speakers on demand, which seemingly allows us to fit the Lord into our busy schedules rather than organizing our lives around Him. However, technology that was made to get the gospel outside the walls of the church or provide additional instruction is no replacement for the Body of Christ.

God created each of us for fellowship with Himself and with other believers. So no matter what reason you might have for separating yourself from the Body of Christ, know that it pales in comparison to why God wants you involved in the church. You need love, encouragement, fellowship, accountability, and a spiritual outlet—and it's through other believers that God provides those things. It is for this reason that Life Principle 28 instructs, *No Christian has ever been called to "go it alone" in his or her walk of faith.*

What the Bible Says

1. Read Acts 6:8–15. What was Stephen accused of doing?

2. Read Acts 7:51–60. What did Stephen condemn the Jewish leaders for doing (see verses 51–52)? What did they do to him (see verses 58–60)?

3. Read Acts 8:1–4. What happened after Stephen's death? How did some Christians respond to the persecution (see verse 4)?

4. Read Hebrews 10:19–25. Why should believers worship God openly and with confidence (see verses 19–21; also see 4:14–16)?

5. What is our confidence based on in all situations (see verses 23, 35–36)? Why are we to meet together regularly (see verses 24–25; see also 3:12–14)?

Stir up in the New Testament means *to incite or stimulate.* We are to encourage and motivate others to be faithful to God. In the same way, Paul admonished Timothy to "stir up the gift of God which is in you. . . . For God has not given us a spirit of fear, but of power and of love and of a sound mind" (2 Timothy 1:6–7).

What It Means

The Jewish community was close knit. They shared ancestry, land, traditions, and a center of worship. However, when Jews began to believe in Jesus as their Messiah, they were disowned and persecuted by their loved ones and neighbors. Some were scattered throughout the world, while others remained in Jerusalem to weather the storm. All must have been intensely aware of the danger of suffering persecution. Yet the writer of Hebrews admonished them to encourage one another and remain steadfast in their faith (see Hebrews 3:13). They needed to draw confidence from other believers, and so do you—especially during the most difficult times. Other Christians will help you grow in your faith, and they will give you the love and support that you need to face the challenges ahead.

Life Examples

1. Read 1 John 3:13–19. Why should we not be surprised when the world opposes us (see verse 13; also see John 15:17–19)?

2. How does our unconditional love for one another show that we belong to Christ and are saved (see verse 14; also see 1 John 4:7–11)?

3. When we refuse to show love to other believers, why is it a condemnation against us (see verses 14–15; see also 1 John 4:20–21)?

4. What should we be willing to do for other believers (see verse 16; also see John 15:13)? What impact does this have on our opinions, prejudices, and biases?

5. What does this passage admonish about sharing with those in need (see verses 17–19; also see James 2:15–17)?

"Love one another; as I have loved you. . . . By this all will know that you are My disciples, if you have love for one another" (John 13:34–35).

Living the Principle

Do you find it easy to open up to other people? Do you consider yourself a loner or are you naturally drawn to others? Regardless of your personal makeup, you need to understand how important it is for you to be part of the church. This will be more challenging for some than for others, but being involved in a Bible-believing congregation is indispensable for *all* Christians.

This is because no one who is bombarded by worldly pressures and ungodly influences can stand by himself or herself for long. Either you will be destroyed by the stress or you will drift away from the faith. Also, you will miss out on the abundant life that God planned for you, because an important part of expressing that life is showing unconditional love to other believers and receiving it from them in return. You need to be involved in a local church—one that will encourage you, keep you accountable, challenge you to grow, help you to express your spiritual gifts, and feed you the meat of God's Word. Remember, the body of Christ isn't complete without you, so don't wait any longer to fulfill the role that you were created for.

Your participation in a local church protects
your personal fellowship with God.

How will you live out Life Principle 28 this week? Consider your current involvement in your local church and think about ways that you could serve if you are not already doing so. Then spend some time in prayer, asking God to draw you into intimate communion with Himself and to transform your life so that you can affect the world for the sake of His kingdom.

Life Lessons to Remember

- Meeting regularly with other believers helps to spur you in your faith (see Hebrews 10:24).
- Fellowship with other Christians will help to safeguard you against drifting (see Hebrews 3:13).
- You have a responsibility to use your gifts to encourage other believers (see 1 Peter 4:10).

LIFE PRINCIPLE 29

You Learn More in Your Valley Experiences than on Your Mountaintops

My brethren, take the prophets, who spoke in the name of the Lord, as an example of suffering and patience.

JAMES 5:10

Life's Questions

Many of the Life Principles are focused on how you respond to adversity. You could say this reflects the amount of adversity that believers face. However, it's primarily due to the fact that the low points in your life are much better teachers than your high points.

In Psalm 23:4, David wrote, "Yea, though I walk through the valley of the shadow of death, I will fear no evil; for You are with me." When you are in the valley, it may seem the walls are closing in around you and there is no escape. You may think, *Is this it? Is this all there is? Is this the end of my story?* But be encouraged: the valley is not the end. In fact, God may just be taking you through the valley to instruct you on what you need to know so you can reach—and truly appreciate—the mountaintops.

Things *will* change because God's will for you is "good and acceptable and perfect" (Romans 12:2). However, right now, there could be something in the valley that God wants you to learn. So consider how He is working in your life as you embrace Life Principle 29: *You learn more in your valley experiences than on your mountaintops.*

What the Bible Says

1. Read James 1:1–8. To whom is this letter written (see verse 1)? Why were they to be joyful in their trials (see verses 2–3)?

⟨⟨⟨ ∽ꝺꞎ ⟩⟩⟩

James is writing to the Jewish Christians that were described in Life Principle 28, who were driven from Jerusalem by the persecution of the Jewish authorities (see Acts 8:1–4). They were away from their homes and families—and not welcomed by their new communities.

2. Why is patience such an important characteristic? How can believers remain patient in difficult situations (see verses 4–5; also see Proverbs 2:2–8)?

3. Read James 5:7–11. What are believers to look forward to seeing (see verse 7)?

4. Why do you think grumbling against others increases when we're under pressure? How can we avoid complaining when we're in a difficult situation (see verse 9)?

5. Why is remembering the prophets—such as Moses, Samuel, Isaiah, Habakkuk, and others—encouraging to us (see verses 10–11; also see Romans 15:4)?

Sometimes God allows us to go without any earthly or
human comfort so that we will turn completely to Him.

What It Means

There are two words in the New Testament for *patience*. The first has to do with difficult circumstances and means to *stay the course or endure*. The second has to do with how we relate to other people. It means *to stay away from rage or furious outbursts*. The believers in the early church were enduring persecution and starting to turn on one another. So

James admonishes them to be patient and trust God. He writes, "We count them blessed who endure . . . the Lord is very compassionate and merciful" (James 5:11). Perhaps your trials are also exposing areas of anger, bitterness, or unforgiveness and you are finding it difficult to persevere. If so, you are starting to understand what God wants you to learn through your trial. Remember, you will be blessed if you endure, so embrace what He is teaching you.

Life Examples

1. Read James 5:13–16. How do your trials help you grow closer to others and to God?

2. Read 1 Kings 17:1 and 18:1. How long did the land go without rain?

3. Read 1 Kings 18:41–45. What did Elijah say would happen (see verse 41)?

4. How many times did Elijah tell his servant to go and check for rain? How did God answer Elijah's prayer (see verses 43–45)?

5. Read James 5:17–18. How can knowing that Elijah is just like you help you when you're in the valley?

Living the Principle

Whenever you experience adversity, it is because God wants to show you His power and love. He may be getting your attention to free you from some emotional bondage or destructive habits. There may be an attitude or behavior in your life that is hindering His work that He needs to eliminate. Perhaps there is some precious quality that He wants to develop in you.

Whatever the reason for the trial, God never means it for your harm. Rather, He means it for your good, so that you can become everything that you were created to be and experience His abundant blessings. Therefore, respond in the way that honors Him. Stay close to Him in prayer and through His Word—obeying whatever He tells you to do. Learn through your valley experiences so that God can prepare you for the mountaintops, because your story is not over. The best is still to come.

═══════ ⟳ ═══════

"Yea, though I walk through the valley of the shadow
of death, I will fear no evil; for You are with me; Your
rod and Your staff, they comfort me" (Psalm 23:4).

═══════════════════════════

How will you live out Life Principle 29 this week? Think about the valleys that you've been experiencing lately and what God might be teaching you through them. Then spend some time in prayer, asking God to draw you into intimate communion with Himself and to transform your life so that you can affect the world for the sake of His kingdom.

Life Lessons to Remember

- Adversity gets your attention (see Psalm 77:2).
- Adversity leads to self-examination (see Psalm 77:6–12).
- Adversity leads to a change in behavior (see Psalm 119:67).

LIFE PRINCIPLE 30

An Eager Anticipation of the Lord's Return Keeps You Living Productively

"And behold, I am coming quickly, and My reward is with Me, to give to every one according to his work."

REVELATION 22:12

Life's Questions

What would you do if you knew that Jesus was returning in just a few hours? The question is not a frivolous exercise in speculation—it may be the prompt you need to examine your Christian walk. Would you be happy about Christ's return and prepare for the celebration? Or would you want to clean up some aspects of your life before He arrived?

The early church lived in eager anticipation of Jesus' return. Some of the believers had been close followers of Christ and were eager to be in His presence again. Others had heard the apostles speak of being with Jesus, and they could hardly wait to see Him face-to-face. There was great enthusiasm in the early church for Christ's return—it was frequently the topic of the believers' conversations because of the hope and joy it stirred within them.

The Second Coming of Christ should also inspire rejoicing and expectancy in believers today as well. After all, 1 Thessalonians 4:16–17 tells us, "The Lord Himself will descend from heaven with a shout. . . . And the dead in Christ will rise first. Then we who are alive and remain shall be caught up together with them in the clouds to meet the Lord in the air." When the Lord returns, He is coming to take you to your new home in heaven—to the place that He has prepared especially for you (see John 14:1–3). It is going to be a wonderful time, and you don't want any regrets to taint your happy reunion with the Lord. This is why Life Principle 30 admonishes, *An eager anticipation of the Lord's return keeps you living productively.*

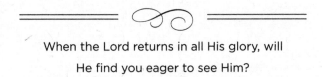

When the Lord returns in all His glory, will
He find you eager to see Him?

What the Bible Says

1. Read Matthew 24:36–44. How did Noah know that the flood was coming (see verses 37–39; also see Genesis 6:13–22)? Who else knew?

2. What kinds of activities will people be doing when Jesus returns (see verses 40–41)?

3. Why should you be watchful for Christ's return, even though you don't know when He is coming (see verses 42–44)?

4. Read Matthew 24:45–51. What happened to the servant who was hard at work preparing for the master's return? What happened to the evil servant?

5. How should believers prepare for Christ's return (see verse 46; also see 1 Thessalonians 5:2–11)? Whom do you need to warn about the consequences of ignoring the Lord's return (see verses 50–51)?

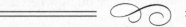

At the Great White Throne Judgment (see Revelation 20:11–15), everyone is judged according to whether or not they've accepted Christ as their Savior. Those who have not will be cast into the lake of fire. Those who have been redeemed will be welcomed into heaven. However, believers will also face an assessment of their works at "the judgment seat of Christ" (see 1 Corinthians 3:11–15; 2 Corinthians 5:9–10).

What It Means

You may be thinking, *Even during Jesus' time, they thought that He was going to return quickly. The Lord's return is probably a lot farther off than we think. We have plenty of time.* However, that is an extremely unwise way to live. You have no idea when God will call you home to heaven—by His return or by some other means. You also don't know when He will require the souls of your loved ones (see Luke 12:20). None of us are promised tomorrow (see James 4:13–15). You always need to remember that you may see the Lord at any minute, because that can keep you motivated to serve Him with all of your heart, mind, soul, and strength.

Life Examples

1. Read Revelation 22:1–5. What will heaven be like (see verses 1–2)? What will believers do there (see verses 3–5)?

2. Read Revelation 22:6–21. Does this passage anticipate a long or short amount of time before the Lord returns (see verses 6–7)? Explain.

3. What is Christ's promise to those who serve Him faithfully (see verses 12–14)?

<hr>

"There shall by no means enter it anything that defiles, or causes an abomination or a lie, but only those who are written in the Lamb's Book of Life" (Revelation 21:27).

<hr>

4. You are the church—the *bride* of Christ. Have you bid everyone you know to "'Come!' . . . Let him who thirsts come . . . take the water of life freely" (see verse 17)?

5. What will your reaction be when Christ returns (see verse 20)?

Living the Principle

Christ's Second Coming should not be just a far off hope for you. It should be a daily reminder that God is *always* active in your life. The Lord leaves you on earth after you are saved for two main reasons. The first is to grow spiritually in oneness with Him. The second is to lead others to a saving knowledge of Jesus Christ. Is that what you've been busy doing? Have you been seeking and serving Him, remembering the reward that awaits you?

It is good to keep Jesus' return at the forefront of your mind so that when you do finally meet Him, you can be just as glad to see Him as He is to see you. So be motivated! Rejoice! Live your life to the fullest and set your eyes and heart firmly on the promise of Christ's return. He has prepared a great reward and a wonderful home for you in heaven. Therefore, be strong—diligently working and expectantly watching for His return—because one day, probably sooner than you expect, you are going to see Him face-to-face.

How will you live out Life Principle 30 this week? Consider how you feel about the Second Coming of Christ. Celebrate His presence with others in the body of Christ and talk about how you can watch for His return and live faithful lives that will please Him. Then spend some time in prayer, asking God to draw you into intimate communion with Himself and to transform your life so that you can affect the world for the sake of His kingdom.

Life Lessons to Remember

- You are to watch for the Lord's return (see Ezekiel 33:7; Mark 13:32–33).
- You are to work as if the Lord were returning soon (see Matthew 9:37–38; 24:45–47).
- You are to eagerly anticipate the Lord's return (see Isaiah 62:11–12).

LEADER'S GUIDE

Thank you for your willingness to lead your group through the *30 Life Principles Study Guide*. The rewards of being a leader are different from those of participating; and as you lead, you will find your own walk with Jesus deepened by this experience. During this study, you and your group members will explore thirty Life Principles in the Bible and how you should respond to them as followers of Christ. There are several elements in this leader's guide that will help you as you structure your study and reflection time, so follow along and take advantage of each one.

Before You Begin

Before your first meeting, make sure the group participants have a copy of this study guide so they can follow along and have their answers written ahead of time. Alternately, you can hand out the guides at your first meeting and give the group members some time to look over the material and ask any preliminary questions. During your first meeting, be sure to send a sheet around the room and have the members write down their names, phone numbers, and email addresses so you can keep in touch with them during the week.

Generally, the ideal size for a group is between eight to ten people, which ensures everyone has time to participate in the discussions. If you have more people, you might want to break up the main group into smaller subgroups. Encourage those who attend the first meeting to commit to attending for the duration of the study, as this will help the group members get to know each other, create stability for the group, and help you know how to prepare each week.

Each lesson begins with a brief introduction to the principle that you and your group members will be studying. As you begin your time together, consider opening with an "icebreaker" question to get the group members thinking about the topic you will discuss. Ask people to share their initial thoughts on the subject, but ask them to keep their answers brief. Ideally, you want everyone in the group to get a chance to answer the question, so try to keep the responses to a minute or less. If you have talkative group members, make sure to state up front that everyone needs to limit his or her answer to one minute.

During your group discussion time, the members should draw off the answers they wrote down to the questions during the week. So encourage them to always complete these exercises ahead of the group meetings. Also, invite them to bring any questions and insights they uncovered while they were reading and studying the Bible to your next meeting—especially if they had a breakthrough moment or didn't understand something they read.

Weekly Preparation

As the group leader, there are a few things you can do to prepare for each meeting:

- *Be familiar with the material in the lesson.* Make sure you understand the content of each lesson so you know how to structure the group time and are prepared to lead the group discussion.
- *Decide which questions you want to discuss.* Depending on how much time you have each week, you may not be able to reflect on every question. Select specific questions you feel will evoke the best discussion.

- *Take prayer requests.* At the end of your discussion, be sure to take prayer requests from your group members and then pray for one another.
- *Pray for your group.* Pray for your group members throughout the week and ask that God would lead them as they study His Word.
- *Bring extra supplies to your meeting.* The members should bring their own pens for writing notes, but it's a good idea to have extras available for those who forget. You may also want to bring paper and additional Bibles.

Note that in many cases, there will not be a "right" answer to any question. Answers will vary, especially when the group members are being asked to share their personal experiences.

Structuring the Discussion Time

You will need to determine with your group how long you want to meet each week so you can plan your time accordingly. Generally, most groups like to meet for either ninety minutes or two hours, so you could use one of the following schedules:

Section	90 Minutes	120 Minutes
Welcome: members arrive and get settled	15 minutes	20 minutes
Icebreaker: discuss an opening icebreaker-type question with the group	15 minutes	20 minutes
Discussion: discuss the Bible study questions you selected ahead of time	50 minutes	60 minutes
Prayer / Closing: pray together as a group and dismiss	10 minutes	20 minutes

As the group leader, it is up to you to keep track of the time and keep things moving according to your schedule. If your group is having a good discussion, don't feel the need to stop and move on to the next question. Remember, the purpose is to pull together ideas and share unique insights on the lesson. Encourage everyone to participate, but don't be concerned if certain group members are quieter. They may just be internally reflecting on the questions and need time to process their ideas before they can share them.

Group Dynamics

Leading a group study can be a rewarding experience for you and your group members—but that doesn't mean there won't be challenges. Discussions can get off track. Certain members may feel uncomfortable in discussing topics that they consider very personal and might be afraid of being called on. Some members might have disagreements on specific issues. To help prevent these scenarios, consider establishing the following ground rules:

- If someone has a question that may seem off topic, suggest that it is discussed at another time, or ask the group if they are okay with addressing that topic.
- If someone asks a question to which you do not know the answer, confess that you don't know and move on. If you feel comfortable, you can invite the other group members to give their opinions or share their comments based on personal experience.
- If you feel like a couple of people are talking much more than others, direct questions to people who may not have shared yet. You could even ask the more dominating members to help draw out the quiet ones.
- When there is a disagreement, encourage the members to process the matter in love. Invite members from opposing sides

to evaluate their opinions and consider the ideas of the other members. Lead the group through Scripture that addresses the topic and look for common ground.

When issues arise, encourage your group to follow these words from Scripture: "Love one another" (John 13:34), "If it is possible, as much as it depends on you, live peaceably with all men" (Romans 12:18), "Whatever things are true . . . noble . . . pure . . . lovely . . . if there is any virtue and if there is anything praiseworthy—meditate on these things" (Philippians 4:8), and "Be swift to hear, slow to speak, slow to wrath" (James 1:19). This will make your group time more rewarding and beneficial for everyone who attends.

Thank you again for your willingness to lead your group. May God reward your efforts and dedication, equip you to guide your group in the weeks ahead, and make your time together in *30 Life Principles* fruitful for His kingdom.

Also Available from Charles F. Stanley

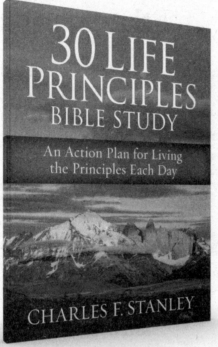

9780310082521   Softcover

30 LIFE PRINCIPLES BIBLE STUDY

An Action Plan for Living the Principles Each Day

During his many years of ministry, Dr. Charles Stanley has faithfully highlighted the 30 life principles that have guided him and helped him to grow in his knowledge, service, and love of God. In this Bible study, you will explore each of these principles in depth and learn how to make them a part of your everyday life. As you do, you will find yourself growing in your relationship with Christ and on the road to the future God has planned for you.

Available now at your favorite bookstore.

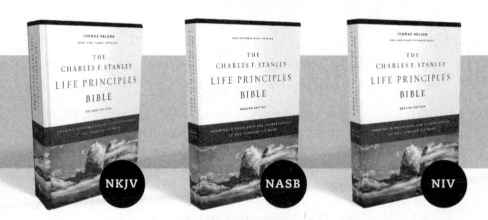

Also Available in the
CHARLES F. STANLEY
Bible Study Series

Each study draws on Dr. Stanley's many years of
teaching the guiding principles found in God's Word,
showing how we can apply them in practical ways to
every situation we face. This edition of the series has
been completely revised and updated, and includes
two brand-new lessons from Dr. Stanley.

Available now at your favorite bookstore.
More volumes coming soon.

The Charles F. Stanley Bible Study Series is a unique
approach to Bible study, incorporating biblical truth,
personal insights, emotional responses,
and a call to action.

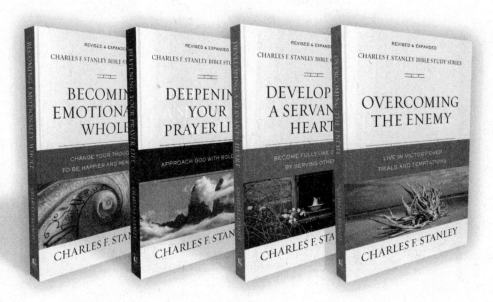

THOMAS NELSON
® Since 1798

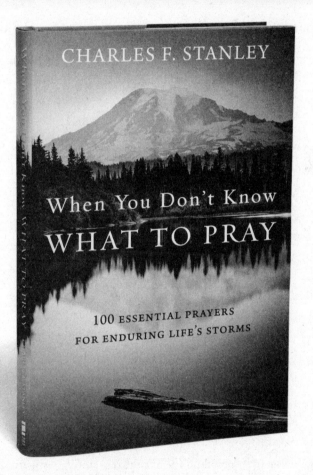